"Combining elements of history, theology, and autobiography, Tim Suttle has written a thought-provoking book that serves as a fresh assessment of Walter Rauschenbusch for the twenty-first-century church. In an age when many Christians use labels such as 'evangelical' and 'liberal' in an uncritical fashion, Suttle calls upon his audience to reflect on how a recovery of the past can lead to a fresh understanding of Christianity today. While written primarily with an evangelical audience in mind, Suttle's study provides a welcome perspective not only on Walter Rauschenbusch and the social gospel, but on how Christianity in America might unfold over the course of the next several decades."

—CHRISTOPHER EVANS
author of *Liberalism Without Illusions: Renewing an American Christian Tradition*

"Every once in a while, as we journey in faith, we will discover the kind of guide who not only helps us find our way, but our voice. Tim Suttle has not only found his way further into God's Kingdom, but he has discovered his own voice by rediscovering a like-minded pastor, theologian, and fellow traveler, in Walter Rauschenbusch. Today, in the footsteps of Rauschenbusch, Tim has found a way to 'reconnect' the personal nature of the Gospel that has become unhinged from the Gospel's corporate and communal nature in the Church of Jesus Christ. Every page of this book burns with the fervent love of God, and immediately, one begins to hear in the infectious words of a compassionate pastor, the unswerving conviction of a prophet, beckoning the whole 'people of God,' and not just the wandering individuals of the Church with their private experience(s) of grace, to join together in the transforming power of God's mission to reconcile the whole world. After all, says Tim, 'the nexus of the personal and corporate is where all the power is.' Yes, a recovery of the Gospel is underway in the Church because these two faithful pastors and prophetic voices have already seen ahead of the rest of us, and now, they are calling the Church to 'run further up and further in' the Kingdom of God."

—K. STEVE MCCORMICK
William M. Greathouse Chair of Wesleyan-Holiness Theology
Nazarene Theological Seminary

"In this remarkable and enjoyable book Tim Suttle draws on the theology of Walter Rauschenbusch in offering a holistic account of the Gospel that is truly good news for the world. In so doing he reminds us that the invitation to follow Jesus and participate in the mission of God involves all that we are in an effort to create a society in which the will of God is done on earth as it is in heaven."

—JOHN R. FRANKE
author of *Manifold Witness: The Plurality of Truth*

"*An Evangelical Social Gospel?* is a probing and passionate call to Christians and churches to move beyond our one-sided individual relationship with God to equally include relationship with others and responsibility for the wider community. Suttle, using the writings and life of Rauschenbush and his own disquiet as a pastor, stirs us to discomfort at our self-centered complacency and co-option by culture, and moves us to redefine 'thy Kingdom come on earth as in heaven' as a call to relationships and transformation of our communities. Transformation goes beyond charity to seeking change in the unjust social structures (public education, prisons, etc). An exciting, challenging, biblically based read that will change your faith, thinking, and action."

—MARY NELSON
Founder
Bethel New Life, CCDA

An Evangelical Social Gospel?

An Evangelical Social Gospel?

Finding God's Story in the Midst of Extremes

TIM SUTTLE

▲ CASCADE *Books* · Eugene, Oregon

Cascade Books
An Imprint of Wipf and Stock Publishers
199 W. 8th Ave., Suite 3
Eugene, OR 97401

www.wipfandstock.com

ISBN 13: 978-1-61097-541-4

Cataloging-in-Publication data:

Suttle, Timothy L.

An evangelical social gospel? : finding God's story in the midst of extremes / Timothy L. Suttle.

xviii + 106 p. ; 23 cm. — Includes bibliographical references.

ISBN 13:978-1-61097-541-4

1. Evangelicalism—United States. 2. Social Gospel. 3. Rauschenbusch, Walter, 1861–1918. I. Title.

BX6495 R3 S75 2011

Manufactured in the U.S.A.

For Kristin, Nicholas, and Lewis—

whose love is a sure sign of the Kingdom.

Dear friends, let us love one another, for love comes from God. Everyone who loves has been born of God and knows God. Whoever does not love does not know God, because God is love. This is how God showed his love among us: He sent his one and only Son into the world that we might live through him. This is love: not that we loved God, but that he loved us and sent his Son as an atoning sacrifice for our sins. Dear friends, since God so loved us, we also ought to love one another. No one has ever seen God; but if we love one another, God lives in us and his love is made complete in us.

This is how we know that we live in him and he in us: He has given us of his Spirit. And we have seen and testify that the Father has sent his Son to be the Savior of the world. If anyone acknowledges that Jesus is the Son of God, God lives in them and they in God. And so we know and rely on the love God has for us.

God is love. Whoever lives in love lives in God, and God in them. This is how love is made complete among us so that we will have confidence on the day of judgment: In this world we are like Jesus. There is no fear in love. But perfect love drives out fear, because fear has to do with punishment. The one who fears is not made perfect in love.

We love because he first loved us. Whoever claims to love God yet hates a brother or sister is a liar. For whoever does not love their brother and sister, whom they have seen, cannot love God, whom they have not seen. And he has given us this command: Anyone who loves God must also love their brother and sister.

—1 John 4:7–21

Contents

Foreword

Last year I received an email from a young minister that contained the unlikely introduction: "I'm a pastor, a student at Nazarene Theological Seminary in Kansas City, and a fan of Walter Rauschenbusch." And so began my journey with Rev. Tim Suttle, whose remarkable book you hold in your hand.

Why was Tim's introduction so unlikely? Not for itself alone, but because the more I learned about Mr. Suttle and his evangelical upbringing, his Christian rock fame, and his successful nondenominational Church plantings, the more I became aware that we were—supposedly—from two different "camps" in the theological divide that had separated Christians like Tim and me for a long time.

As the narrative goes, one hundred years ago (give or take a decade) American Protestants split into two oddly opposing factions with Mainline churches on one side and Evangelicals on the other. Common wisdom held that the mainline churches only cared about social justice and evangelicals only cared about individual salvation. Each side painted the other with increasingly broad and clumsy strokes, resulting in mutual suspicion and even adversarial relationships.

One of the figures who became associated with this parting of the ways was my great-grandfather, Walter Rauschenbusch. Walter was born into a Christian household and followed the family tradition of pursuing a seminary education and entering the ministry. In 1886, he took a church in the appropriately named "Hell's Kitchen" of New York City. Rauschenbusch's goal was, in his words, "to save souls," and he went about this work with industry and conviction. Yet as he offered spiritual pastoral care to his congregation he was confronted with the reality of the physical and psychological suffering of the working poor of his church. It was a time in America when if you did not have enough money to eat, you went hungry; if you did not have enough money to pay rent, you were out in the cold; and if you did not have enough money for medicine, death was often the result. Rauschenbusch spent too much of his time consoling those who had lost their loved ones only because they were poor. When speaking about his ministry in Hell's Kitchen, Rauschenbusch lamented: "Oh the children's funerals! They gripped my heart—the small boxes. I always left thinking—why did these children have to die?"

This fundamental question of the church's relation to physical suffering and degradation—"the small boxes" of deaths that happened on account of poverty and deprivation—guided Rauschenbusch's life and ministry. With a desire to understand the Gospel teachings on tragic injustice that he had encountered, Walter went back to the Bible and wrote this parable reflecting his process of discovery:

> A man was walking through the woods in springtime. The air was thrilling and throbbing with the passion of little hearts, with the love wooing, the parent pride, the deadly fear of the birds. But the man never noticed that there was a bird in the woods. He was a botanist and was looking for plants. A man read through the New Testament. He felt no vibrations of social hope in the preaching of John the Baptist and in the shouts of the crowd when Jesus entered Jerusalem. Jesus knew human nature when he reiterated: "He that hath ears to hear, let him hear." We see in the Bible what we have been taught to see there.

Once Walter had his eyes opened by the suffering of his congregation (an experience he likened to being born again), he saw that the Jesus of the Bible had offered good news to the poor and oppressed in his time, and continue to offer that message to the poor of Rauschenbusch's own congregation. Rauschenbusch focused on the kingdom of God which was meant to "come, on earth as it is in heaven," founded on love and equality. In speaking about the Lord's Prayer, Walter wrote: "There is no request here that we be saved from earthliness and go to heaven, rather we pray here that heaven may be duplicated on earth through the moral and spiritual transformation of humanity, both in its personal and corporate life."

Rauschenbusch re-approached scripture and tradition with the suffering children on his heart and discovered that Jesus's message of redemption had always contained both the personal and the social dimensions—both physical and spiritual redemption were included in the grand invitation of Jesus into the kingdom of God. Rauschenbusch's whole life, ministry, and writing was all dedicated to creating a society that more closely reflected Jesus's vision of the kingdom of God.

Unfortunately, many Christians thought that any talk of transforming society was a distraction from the individual salvation they believed was at the heart of the Gospel, and so Christians began to take sides. Walter was grieved by the fracture of evangelicals from liberals that had already begun during his lifetime. Rauschenbusch always thought of his work as evangelism, and considered the social Gospel an addition to, not a replacement of, the Gospel upon which he had been raised.

A century later there is a family reunion in American Christianity, and the book you hold in your hand is one more testimony to our reconciliation. What joy it must give my great-grandfather that Pastor Suttle came across his writing and was transformed by the call of the kingdom of God. And Tim is not alone! Over the past few years I have had the pleasure of working side by side with Evangelical leaders and young people, whom I have come to regard as long lost sisters and brothers, separated by an unfortunate divorce that we did not create. Many evangelicals, especially younger ones, are more and more interested in the social message of Jesus. Indeed, most of my invitations to speak these days are from Christian colleges whose students are fired up about questions of social justice because of their love for Jesus.

At the same time, we in the mainline churches are looking to be revived through a deep commitment to the Christian life, and a personal connection with God that is more traditionally associated with our Evangelical sisters and brothers. We are becoming more interested in the spiritual gifts of our tradition and attempting disciplined spiritual engagement with Jesus, even as we continue the call for social salvation.

This book is written with an Evangelical audience in mind, and will certainly captivate, challenge and hopefully enrich those of you from that tradition. But the book is equally pertinent to liberal Mainline Protestants, some of whom may be unaware of the Evangelical roots of our own tradition. Both Mainline and Evangelicals will be "turned on" by the spiritual vigor of Rev. Suttle, whose faith comes through on every page, and who is striving to follow Jesus into full engagement with the world.

A piece of advice that I gave to Tim when he visited me was to use Rauschenbusch as inspiration, but to truly make this book his own reflection on Jesus, the kingdom of God, and authentic discipleship. The result is a book that has theological breadth and depth and a remarkably fresh take on fundamental tenets of our faith. Tim helps us to remember how Rauschenbusch continues to be relevant in today's difficult world.

However he is not merely restating. In his synthesis, he is creating a new theology that is challenging and inspiring.

One of the great pleasures of reading Rauschenbusch is his witty writing style and his ability with metaphor such as: "Wealth—to use a homely illustration—is to a nation what manure is to a farm. If the farmer spreads it evenly over the soil, it will enrich the whole. If he should leave it in heaps, the land would be impoverished and under the rich heaps the vegetation would be killed."

Likewise, Suttle will make you smile with his entertaining writing style and illustrations. Take this one for example: "Belief is a slippery concept. Just imagine you are pulled over by a police officer for driving seventy-five where the limit is fifty-five miles per hour. He asks you why you were driving so fast. Would you say, 'I know the speed limit is only fifty-five, I believe that in my heart. In fact, I was going fifty-five in my heart, it's just that I was in a hurry on the outside!' Once the officer stops laughing, you're going to get a ticket. Faith is like that. It's not simply an inner phenomenon."

This is a book that is a journey, and we are walking with the author every step of the way. A true pastor, Tim does not rush ahead assuming we will catch up eventually. Instead he guides us through the transformation of his own thinking, using compelling examples from his own life and those of his friends. For instance, he tells the story of a writer in Amsterdam who was struck by the experiencing of witnessing a group of tourists taunt a young woman who was working as a prostitute. The writer raged: "These aren't animals in a zoo. This is a human tragedy. What's wrong with you people? This is somebody's daughter, somebody's sister, somebody's mother."

We are made to wonder: how will the gospel make a difference in the life of the girl in the cage in Amsterdam? The suffering of the girl echoes the little boxes of the funerals of children that my great-grandfather wrestled with over a century ago. How does the Gospel matter in the world here and now? The challenge this question presents remains crucial today when so many people still go without the basic dignity of food and shelter—even in America, the richest nation on earth.

My prayer for all of us is that we continue to grapple with that question of how the Gospel matters, and join one another as laborers in God's kingdom on earth as it is in heaven. Thanks Tim, for giving us this book as an enlightening and encouraging place to start.

Paul Brandeis Raushenbush
Princeton University, 2011

Acknowledgments

This book owes its original impetus to Dr. John Knight, and his class on early twentieth century theology at Nazarene Theological Seminary. Dr. Knight made Walter Rauschenbusch's *A Theology for the Social Gospel* required reading (a brave thing to do in an evangelical seminary), and I will be forever grateful for that introduction. My thinking concerning Rauschenbusch, missional theology, and the Kingdom of God has been informed, stimulated, and nurtured by many great mentors and teachers. Were it not for the encouragement of Steve McCormick, Andy Johnson, and Ron Benefiel, I would have never had the courage to undertake this project. They cannot be held accountable for what follows here, but none of this would have materialized were it not for their friendship, guidance, and skill as teachers. Steve McCormick has gone above and beyond what a professor should be expected to do in order to help me cut my theological teeth. He encouraged me to find my voice and reminded me that writing is mainly about fighting your own demons. For his great scholar's mind and pastor's heart I will be forever thankful. Isaac Anderson edited the book proposals for this project. He helped me to refine the scope of the book and listened to me blather on about Walter Rauschenbusch for many a night. I remember several conversations during which Isaac reminded me the good news must always be personal. Those conversations have undoubtedly found their way into this work. My good friend and colleague Scott Savage has pushed me to think theologically and integrate theology and the practice of ministry. I have road-tested nearly all of my illustrations and major points with Scott, who helped me to pick them apart and refine my thinking. Scott has offered critique and encouragement in equal parts and has made the writing process a little less lonely. Thank you to Ryan Green, Todd Way, and Chaim Carstens for the many trips to Denny's and for letting me take more than my turn to talk. Thank you to my parents and siblings. Your lives, lived in fidelity to the gospel, bear witness to the rich heritage we all inherited from the Suttle and Stith families.

This book's argument owes so much to so many people. I'm very thankful to Paul Raushenbush, who let me sit on Walter and Pauline Rauschenbusch's couch in the Brandeis summer home and gave me the pre-game inspiration and direction I needed to launch into this project. Paul has been gracious with his time and lavish with his encouragement and I've thought about him and his family often while writing this book. That the Rauschenbusch legacy of Christian social activism lives on, even to the present generations of the family, is a testament both to the greatness of Walter Rauschenbusch and to the integrity and purpose with which they have all lived their lives. I must say thank you also to Stanley Hauerwas and Brian McLaren for their encouraging reviews of the rough draft. I am indebted to Paul Minus and Christopher Evans for teaching me about Rauschenbusch's life. Dr. Evans took the time to correspond with me about the book, and encouraged me to write it. His biography of Rauschenbusch, *The Kingdom Is Always But Coming*, remains the definitive work on Rauschenbusch's life.

Were it not for the generosity of the Louisville Institute, this book might never have been written. Their Sabbatical Grant for Pastoral Leaders gave me and my family the opportunity and environment we needed in order to make our family's sabbatical and my manuscript production a simultaneous reality. In particular the hospitality and resources they made available during the SGPL Consultation was critical for me. Also thanks to Martha and our friends at the Wellfleet, MA, Public Library, where much of this manuscript was produced. Thanks to Rick and Dawn Mundy and KC Creative. Dawn did the copy-editing for the manuscript.

A special thank you goes to Jeff Suttle and Bill Hill, who read all of my rough drafts and made extensive contributions and suggestions at every stage. You are two of the most intelligent and insightful people I've ever known. You serve as excellent models for how the lay-person should engage in mission. Jeff and Bill both made careful comments on every single chapter, offering brilliant suggestions at critical points in the writing process. They helped me figure out how to say what I actually meant to say. Their friendship and encouragement was matched only by their unselfish dedication of their time. I am so grateful to you both.

It is a true privilege to be a part of the staff, elders, and members of Redemption Church in Olathe, KS. You guys are the stuff church-dreams are made of. I thank you for allowing me to be your pastor, for allowing me the space to read and study and do serious theological reflection without having to leave the local church, and for allowing me to take a sabbatical with my family. Mostly I thank you for your pursuit of the Kingdom of God and for your fidelity toward each other and the Mission of God. I celebrate your love of Christ and the gospel in these pages. I hope this book sounds familiar—because it is an attempt to describe what you already are. You have given me a vision of how the church can be the church. Here's to many, many years of being caught up in the mission of God with the Redemption Church family.

My final thank you is reserved for Kristin, Nicholas, and Lewis Suttle. No one who hasn't done it before can ever fully appreciate what it means to marry a pastor. You bear much of the burden, and get none of the credit. Everything I know about fidelity and faithfulness I've learned from you, Kristin. You are an incredible wife and mother, and you embody all of what this book is about. I thank you for the countless conversations which were forced upon you during the writing process. I don't know how you did it, but you always seemed excited to have them, even when they got in the way of our "normal" lives. Your keen insights, especially after the first few chapters were written, sent the project in a whole different direction. Your constant reading and listening along the way left your fingerprints all over this book, and for that I promise to share all of the royalties with you. To Nicholas and Lewis, I thank you for allowing this book to intrude on upon our vacations, sabbaticals, weekends, and evenings together. You guys are the very definition of unconditional love. I pray that you will never know single a day that you don't feel a part of the people of God, and that you will experience the indescribable joy of peace with God, with yourselves, with other people, and with the world around you. You made our summer of writing, exploring, and playing in Cape Cod a real season of Grace. In my memory you will always be my sweet little boys—Prince Caspian and King Edmund—with toy swords, helmets, and towels wrapped around your shoulders as capes, fighting the enemies of Aslan in the backyard. May you always know how much your parents love you, and may you always pursue God's Kingdom and have courage to run "further up and further in!"

Introduction

I have a friend named Sam. She grew up going to church, and has always been an avid reader and a bit of a theology buff. I used to tell her that she was too rigid and closed off concerning new theological ideas. She used to tell me I was too nutty, and although we were friends, I think she viewed me with suspicion. I used to think Sam saw her theology as if it were a bucket full of little building blocks like the little ones my kids used to play with, the ones that have letters painted on two sides. Sam spent her whole life collecting these little blocks to put in her theological bucket. She'd go to Sunday school and pick up a block. She'd read a book and get another block. All through her life these blocks would come together from all sorts of different places—moms and dads, pastors, youth groups, college bible studies, books, songs, movies—each of them contributing to this theological bucket.

As she grew older, the game shifted for Sam. Somewhere in her early twenties she went from picking up new blocks for her theological bucket to examining the blocks she already had in there. Sam would still try to cram a new block in the bucket every once in awhile, but for the most part she would encounter things which forced her to pull out an old block and take a good hard look at it in order to decide where to fit it back in or whether to discard it altogether. Sam would read a book or see a film and be forced to dig around in the bucket, find the corresponding block and ponder its worth. Then she had to find a way to fit it back into the bucket without messing everything up.

Pretty soon the bucket was crammed to the top and packed tight. And every time she came across something which corresponded to a block in her bucket she had to answer a few important questions: "Is it really worth digging through all of these blocks to consider the worth of any single one? How will I ever get them back inside the bucket if I do this? What happens if they don't fit afterwards?" More often than not, the answer was, "No, it's not worth digging through the bucket, it might mess

1

up my well ordered system." So Sam started to become more and more closed off to things which might challenge her way of thinking.

This worked okay until Sam started to encounter serious pain and suffering. First, she got married, and then her husband cheated on her with a colleague at work. That same year she found out her mom had cancer. Through her divorce and the lengthy illness up until her mom's death, Sam held on to that bucket like it was full of gold bars. She thought it was that bucket full of theology which would get her through. The day her mom died, Sam was alone with her in the hospital room and she bore witness to her mom's passing. That's suffering, and suffering does strange things to a person.

Sam tells the story better than I do, but basically when she got home to an empty house fresh from watching her mother die, the blocks came out of her bucket. Not one-by-one in an orderly fashion, but she unceremoniously dumped the entire bucket on the table.

Here's the weird thing. The moment Sam dumped her theological bucket on the table she realized that there were tons of other blocks already there. They were not hers. She'd never seen them before. Sam discovered that they belonged to people in her community of faith. When she looked up she realized that these people from her community of faith were actually all seated around this same table, crammed elbow to elbow. The table was packed and pieces were falling on the floor and some of her friends were playing catch with them, some were looking at the blocks with magnifying glasses, some were building pyramids; it was crazy. The table was full of people, and blocks, and conversation, and laughter, and tears, and suffering and healing, and tension and freedom.

Life had this way of forcing Sam to open up. She carried that bucket around for so long and she had it packed so tightly that it really wasn't doing her any good. About all she could do with it was swing it wildly to keep dangerous people at bay. It was rigid and closed off and when her husband left and her mom died, the bucket was useless dead weight. When she finally dumped it out she learned that the table was full of life because there were other people there, and new blocks and old were bouncing around like popcorn. She realized her old bucket was really just an illusion. These blocks weren't meant to be carried around in a bucket or wielded as weapons, but for building something beautiful with friends.

I don't think Sam is closed off anymore. And she no longer views me with suspicion. We don't agree on the worth of every theological building block on the table, but we sit at the table together. What Sam learned more than any other thing is that she was never meant to have her own bucket in the first place. She didn't own those blocks, they belong to the people of God. When she closed things off and packed them into a rigid system, they became unable to help her when suffering dragged her into the depths.

Perhaps this is a good metaphor for how theology should happen. It should be like children at play around a table filled with little blocks. Everyone should know that they will never be anything but little children when it comes to theology. The metaphor implies certain freedoms and options for how things can fit together and be organized. We can build all kinds of things. Every child of God around the table contributes. It also implies a certain amount of disorder at all times—after all we're like children. Sometimes we make a mess. It also implies that if you want your blocks back to take with you at the end of the day, you can forget it. The blocks stay on the table, for theology is a corporate enterprise.

God, the loving parent walks around the table and leans over our shoulders and says "Let's build this," or "Let's build that." We join in because we know this loving parent always has great ideas. The metaphor implies community, freedom, trust, guidance, and it implies play.

This all sounds really great until we get to our favorite block: freewill, predestination, penal substitutionary atonement, Eucharist, Baptism, liberalism, or conservativism. These blocks mean different things to different people. Some are considered sacred, some profane. What about our most basic building blocks of what it means to be a person, or a Christian? Are those on the table? What about the most basic question "What is the Gospel?" For many seekers of truth this question is in play. Sadly for many people it is not. What about sin? What about salvation? What about the kingdom of God? It is these rudimentary building blocks which are the focus of this book.

Those are difficult questions to ask and they can be a little scary. But I believe there is a beautiful room in the human heart which only opens from the inside. And it will only open up when we give up our need for answers and just commit ourselves to pursuing the questions. I once heard David Burrell say that there is a huge difference between those who need certitude and those who search for truth. Personally, those who need certitude have always made me a little nervous. But I'm constantly attracted to those who have the courage to pursue the questions.

There is something profound about the Jewish tendency to answer questions with more questions. In the Scriptures we often find Jesus conversing with those who were asking the difficult questions of their day. What's amazing about Jesus is that he seemed to be able to get to the real question behind all of people's other questions. Perhaps one of the most important questions behind all of these questions could be "Do you need certitude or are you searching for truth and understanding?" It is this question you will need to wrestle with as you read this book.

Too many people live their lives as though they have spiritual bulimia. They sporadically binge on ideas and then spit them back up without ever really properly digesting them. After awhile all of the answers they come up with start to sound the same. I think Jesus wants to invite us to this place where we cease with our own agenda and we stop trying to get Jesus to say what we want him to say. Because he's really not interested in telling us what we *want* to hear, he's interested in telling us what we *need* to hear. I did not go looking for most of the things I've written in this book, they just happened to me gradually as I lived among the people of God. There was a time when many of these things would have been offensive to me. But through the conversation at the table—my childish playing with blocks—I have come to see that understanding comes through tension and tension comes through relationships with others who are different from me. This book emerged out of the questions I've been asking with my faith community.

I would like to invite you to come and play with me at the table. Bring your bucket full of blocks and dump it out with mine and some of my friends' that I've brought with me. We're going to have a conversation about life and what God is doing through the church. God is here, God will guide us. God is pleased when we come together and lay it all on the table. Come and play!

1 Rock and Roll, Shotguns, and the Art of Car Maintenance

One of my favorite childhood memories has to be sitting in front of my parents' console stereo listening to records. Forget about iPods and mp3's piped through terrible sounding headphones. This was a real stereo hi-fi, big enough to lie down and take a nap on. It was long and loud with a smooth, elastic, analog tone. I would sit beside it listening over and over to vinyl LP records (or 8-track tapes), by REO Speedwagon, Journey, Kansas, and believe it or not, John Denver. I'd go to the closet and pull out one of my parent's tennis rackets and hold it like a Gibson Gold Top guitar, and check myself out in the reflection from the picture window in our living room. Striking my most rebellious rock star pose, I'd windmill like Pete Townshend and sing my heart out, butchering the words to *Take It on the Run, Baby,* and *Carry on My Wayward Son.* I would lie in front of that giant stereo and stare at the album jackets for hours. I loved looking at the live shots of the bands. I loved pictures of musicians in the studio with their long hair and funky clothes. I wanted to be in those pictures. I wanted to be in the band.

So I started to play, guitar, piano, harmonica, or anything else I could get my hands on. I found that I actually had some natural ability for it. After graduating from college with no prospects, and no marketable skills, I did the most sensible thing I could think of at the time. I started a band. By 1998, my band *Satellite Soul* hand landed a record contract and was travelling and playing full time. We inked the deal and walked into Ardent Studios in Memphis completely wet behind the ears, ready to take our shot at the big-time. Before we knew it our first record was released, our first music video was shot, and the first single was breaking into the top five on the charts. We had no idea what was going on. This wasn't really supposed to happen was it? We were just an indie band playing bars and churches around the Midwest. When it finally sunk in that for some reason God was giving us a platform, we made each other a simple promise: we would make this about something bigger than ourselves and our careers. We wanted it to be about the gospel.

I remember one night later on that same year we were opening for the Newsboys at Universal Studios in Orlando Florida. I was looking out across this sea of people, there had to be eight to ten thousand of them, milling around and talking—just waiting for the show to begin. All of the sudden, the lights went dim and the crowd began to yell that high-pitched sound of pure anticipation. I'll never forget that moment, pregnant with expectation and possibility. We walked on stage to take our places in the dark while the introductions finished. The lights kicked on, the sound came up, I strummed down my Rickenbacker six-string electric, blew into my harmonica, the band kicked in, and we were off to the races. It was magic. Out of everything I've ever done in my musical career, there will be no better musical moment. There's nothing like that first down-beat—the drums, the bass, the guitars all in perfect sync—propelled by the power of a massive sound system and thousands of screaming fans. I was in heaven.

Over the next decade, Satellite Soul played nearly a thousand shows all over the country. We gave our life to the road and to this band which we genuinely thought of as a ministry. Night after night I would tell about Jesus, and how he died to set us free. I would share the good news with people, but over time something strange began to happen. I started to feel like no matter what I said, how we played, or how big the crowd was, our ministry seemed to make little impact on the world. As I developed relationships with other musicians I learned that I was not alone. Most of us struggled with this inescapable sense that the gospel should have more impact on the people we shared it with. The more we played the more we started to feel like nothing we were saying or doing was making any difference at all. Time after time we'd crank up the amps and sing the same songs, tell the same stories, and try desperately to make a connection with people, and make a difference in the world, but I could never escape the nagging feeling I wasn't making any difference at all.

After Satellite Soul stopped touring full time I went on staff with a church in the Kansas City area to help plant a new church in another part of the city. I dove headfirst into that ministry just like I had with Satellite Soul. My wife and I started a family and leveraged everything we had to try and build a church that would make a difference in the world.

After several years of ministry the church seemed like a success from the outside. Yet, when we were honest with each other—from the senior staff down to the marginally involved attendee—all of us were wondering if all of our work was making a difference.

Have you ever felt that way? Have you ever wondered why the gospel we have given our lives to doesn't have more impact on the world? For the past twenty years of my ministry, I've seen people who work hard and live with integrity and purpose. They give their hearts to Christ and raise their families in the church. They volunteer at church and support the ministry financially. They try to invest in friendships in the hope that they might get to share with them the joy they find in a relationship with Christ. They hold nothing back from God or from the church community. They do everything that is ever asked of them, and yet they constantly wonder if anything they are doing is making any difference. Have you ever been frustrated with the fact that you are a part of a church and you give and give and give to that ministry, but it doesn't seem to have much impact on the world? Why is this happening? Why don't we see the good news going forth in power and changing our entire community?

I lived my life in this tension for many years. I've wrestled with the ubiquitous, nagging feeling that with all of the time, money, passion, and creativity we put into communicating the good news to people, we should be seeing the world changing all around us. Our churches, towns, and cities should be catching fire with the life-altering vision of the kingdom of God. But it isn't happening. Why isn't it happening?

What follows here is my possibly lame, certainly limited, yet nevertheless honest and passionate attempt to help the church be more faithful and effective. I don't want people to feel frustrated anymore, as though the sacrifices they are making for their church and for the gospel are not making any difference. I don't want to be frustrated anymore either. I think the good news can change the world just as it did two-thousand years ago. I want us to reconsider the way we talk about the gospel—the good news of God's redemption through Jesus Christ—and begin to conceive and communicate it in a more robust and powerful way.

OF SHOTGUNS AND CAR MAINTENANCE

The Darwin Awards are these hilariously wrong, real-life stories of how people have accidentally caused their own demise; natural selection in real time. I heard a story which should be a nominee, except I don't think the guy died. Admittedly, there are moments for all of us when we are about to try something risky, and we say to ourselves, "I hope this works." This had surely been one of those times, I guess . . . I don't really know, but the story goes like this. A Kitsap County Washington man had been working on his old Lincoln Continental for weeks outside his home. He had apparently been attempting to remove the right rear wheel from the car, but one of the lug nuts was stubbornly stuck in place. It seems the 66-year-old man had tried everything he could think of to loosen that lug nut when, after reaching the pinnacle of frustration, he went inside, got his 12 gauge shot gun, loaded it with buck-shot, and shot the wheel. The Sherriff's report says he fired the shotgun from about an arm's length and was immediately peppered from his chest to his feet with shot and other sorts of debris. "Nobody else was there and he wasn't intoxicated," the Sherriff said.[1] One can always know they've made a huge mistake when those who are trying to explain the incident feel compelled to clarify that the person has not, in fact, been drunk out of their tree. It's a sure sign you have derailed. "He's bound and determined to get that lug nut off," said the Sherriff. You think, really?

Ever used the wrong tool for the job? Just a guess, but I'm thinking rule number one in the art and science of fixing automobiles is that a shotgun is never really helpful. I remember doing the dishes when I was a kid, struggling to get spaghetti sauce off our dinner plates. My mom noticed my frustration and showed me that if I'll use the hottest water my hands can stand, the sauce will come right off. I was so amazed when it worked that I almost enjoyed doing dishes for a few days. Hot water, who knew?

The right tool for the job can be the difference between great success and miserable failure. As a Christian and a pastor, I often think of this maxim as I consider what in the world it is I'm trying to do. I was handed a set of tools when I was very young. Beliefs, doctrines, strategies, and especially stories, which were meant to help me understand the Christian faith, were instilled in me from a very young age. It is the same for most of us who grew up in the evangelical Christian community. These tools were meant to make me a faithful Christian and an effective witness for the gospel. They were supposed to work, and I suppose they did to some

---

1. Associated Press, "Revenge of the Lug Nut."

extent. But you can clean your dishes with cold water, too. It just takes considerably more time and energy. I think perhaps they worked because God works with whatever broken thing God can, not because they were terribly effective or faithful tools. When faced with a particularly sticky lug nut, one might be tempted to reach for the shotgun (which I think we can all agree is a big mistake). It's just a lot more effective if you use the right tool for the job.

I have come to believe American Evangelical Christianity as a whole has been using the wrong tool for the job when it comes to the way we view the Christian gospel, and the way we share that message with the world. The reason can be a little complicated, but it's really, really important to understand. It's complicated because it's *theological* in nature. The word theology is just a ten-cent word which is really two words in one: *theo*, meaning "God," and *ology*, meaning "talk." Theology is "God-talk." The way we talk about God has become problematic, especially when it comes to the way we talk about the gospel itself. The words we use work powerfully to shape our understanding of the gospel, and thus they shape who we are becoming as the people of God.

Over the past few centuries, the way we tell the story of God has changed. It has become overly individualized, reduced to a way of managing the guilt we feel as the result of our sinfulness. This gospel has little or no moral or ethical implications. It makes few demands on our lives right here and now. I find this strange given the emphasis Jesus places on obedience. The gospel which most of us who grew up in the evangelical church were taught—the one we know how to tell—is only part of the story. It's just about how to deal with sin and "go to heaven" when we die. But this is not the major theme of the teachings of Jesus. This "gospel of sin management,"[2] as Dallas Willard calls it, does not do justice to the good news we find in the Scriptures, and thus it doesn't have the desired effect on us, on our communities, and on our world.

Most of us who grew up among evangelicals were taught a gospel which went something like this: Everyone is a sinner, and the punishment for sin is death. Jesus took our punishment on the cross and if we believe in him, receive him as Savior, and invite him into our hearts, we will receive eternal life and go to heaven when we die. That's what we were taught, and for the most part, it is the story we tell. But if we consider it carefully,

2. Willard, *The Divine Conspiracy*, 35.

we will realize that version of the gospel is only about the individual and God. It's about you and Jesus and what you believe about who he is. It is all about each individual winning heaven and immortality through faith in Christ. At its heart, *this version of the gospel is about us getting something we want or need,* i.e., forgiveness and eternal life. It is ultimately selfish and individualistic. It requires very little from us apart from mental assent to certain truth claims about Jesus. It is all about the individual and God, and carries with it few social implications, if any. And in a nation of selfish people who have individualism forced upon them from the day they are born, our faith has become too individualistic as well. The gospel we tell is too individualistic, and has become indistinguishable from the narrative of the culture at large. It should be no wonder it doesn't call people to change.

What if the reason the gospel has become ineffective is that it has been co-opted by individualism? What if our gospel is more about individualized religion than authentic good news? What if the gospel has become so dominated by individualism, that in a country full of individualists, the gospel doesn't stand out as anything different, doesn't ask us to live differently? Maybe this is why we give our lives to try and share the good news with people and are continually frustrated and disappointed with the results. We're not telling the whole story! The truth is hard to hear, but I believe this is true[the version of the gospel most American evangelical Christians tell bears little resemblance to the gospel Jesus preached, nor does it echo the kind of life-altering pursuit of the kingdom which we see at work in the lives of the great saints of the New Testament.]

I wish I could say I've never been frustrated enough to take a shot at this sticky lug nut. I cannot. I've fired in frustration countless times and I typically end up injuring myself in the process. I've handed out my condemnations, and I usually regret it. I've slandered, complained and threatened to leave. But I haven't left because I think deep down I realize this is who I am; these are my people. For better or for worse, I am in and of the tradition of American Evangelicalism. So I don't write this critique as an outsider, but as one who has great love for the evangelical church. However, I am resolved to confront my tradition, even to poke it with a stick because, well, it *is* my tradition. I'm not going anywhere and the truth is we need to rethink a few things. This book is the best way I know to show my love. Wounds of a friend and all . . .

A BREAK IN THE CLOUDS

Here's the problem as clearly as I can state it. For the past few centuries, individualistic conceptions of the gospel have championed some truly good things: the emphasis that every human person can have a personal relationship with God through faith in Christ; the essential nature of personal faith; the priesthood of the believer; the missionary spirit; the consistent appeal to the authority of scripture; the resistance of the absolute power of a corrupt church; and many others. But, the resulting forms and modes of what it means to follow Christ have been overly-geared toward individual salvation and self-enhancement. As a result, the individualistic nature of the gospel has become distorted and overplayed. Individualism has usurped the essential communal and corporate nature of the Christian faith, and the social claims which Jesus makes on the life of his followers have been drowned out and ignored. When this happened the gospel lost its power. <u>?</u> *it wasn't the gospel*

When astronauts take a trip to space, they have to carry their own oxygen. They can't just open up the windows of their spacecraft and get a breath of fresh space air. Space is a vacuum. The air would instantly be sucked out of their lungs, which I'm guessing is not a very good way to go. The lack of oxygen in space means rocket fuel will not burn either. Rocket fuel in and of itself is worthless in space. Without oxygen it cannot burn, it cannot oxidize, and thus cannot propel the spacecraft. If you want your rocket fuel to burn in space, you have to carry your own oxygen with you. Only then can you fire your rockets and get where you are meant to go.

The gospel is like this. It has a personal dimension—just between you and God—and this is a critical piece. It also has a corporate dimension—between you and all of humanity, even the created order—and this is a critical piece as well. You have to have the personal and corporate dimensions working in tandem for the fire to burn and get you where you are meant to go. As oxygen is to rocket fuel in space, so the corporate dimension is to the personal dimension in the Christian gospel. In American Evangelicalism, we have the personal covered, but we are lacking in the corporate understanding of the good news. *The nexus of the personal and corporate is where all the power is.*

The tradition which protected and emphasized the corporate nature of the gospel has often been called the Social Gospel movement. It has been attacked and maligned by evangelicals for a century, sometimes rightfully so, for shunning any mention of personal faith and a relationship with God. But we need to put that behind us. It is time to realize *the gospel is personal for sure, but it is also corporate*. Today, individualistic ideas of what it means to follow Jesus hang like a cloud over the message of Christ we find in the Scriptures. Jesus, following in the footsteps of the prophets who came before him, was very serious about the corporate nature of the gospel. Yet, perhaps in our day and our time there is a moment—a break in the clouds—a chance for us to hear the true gospel which binds us together as the people of God and sends us out in the mission of God. Shouldn't the gospel be good news for the cultures and institutions of all societies, as well as the individual persons? To rediscover the corporate aspect of the gospel will require a clear theological exploration of the gospel in ways that favor the solidarity of all humankind over the primacy of the individual. Maybe if we began to preach the gospel this way, we would discover this is how God has planned it from the very beginning.

As I said, I am writing as an evangelical Christian. If that is not your cup of tea, it is entirely possible this makes absolutely no sense to you so far. Yet I hope the issues I address here will challenge all of us who call ourselves followers of Jesus. The church is on the verge of irrelevancy in our culture, but our problem is not a lack of cultural relevancy as many assume. A few candles, some incense, and a good rock band won't help us here. The problem runs much deeper than that. The problem is the gospel message has been overshadowed and corrupted by the rival god of individualism.

We might pray, "Thy kingdom come, Thy will be done in earth as it is in heaven," but do we really expect it to happen? Do we really mean it? It's time for us to face up to the fact that the limiting reagent in this chemical reaction is not God, it is us. We are the problem. The church is all rocket fuel and no oxygen, and so the way we bear witness to the gospel has become problematic. We are ignoring its communal nature and in so doing we are robbing it of its power.

2 Rugged Individualism, Amsterdam, and Walter Rauschenbusch

Individualism is part of the American narrative. We are the land of the rugged individualist. In America anyone can pull themselves up by their own bootstraps and make their life whatever they want it to be. We celebrate the heroic and elevate those who conquer. This is the shape of the American story. America was started by brave individuals who ventured across the sea to colonize the new world. It was expanded by strong individuals who pushed west across the frontier to settle the lands from New England to California. Our brave leaders came to preeminence in the twentieth century as they toppled Hitler, then soared toward the heavens and put a man on the moon. America is the land of individual rights, individual freedoms, and the great American hero. We celebrate our own virtue when we celebrate George Washington, who could not tell a lie. We celebrate our own bravery when we celebrate Patrick Henry's bold proclamation, "Give me liberty or give me death." Among our most sacred documents is the forceful declaration of our own independence. This is the American story. It is the land where the tales of rugged individualism pass from generation to generation, to fund a virtuous nation.

Evangelicals have been formed in this narrative of individualism, so it should be no surprise that the gospel we tell in America should have an individualistic bent. *But, the story of individualism is not synonymous with the story of Christianity.* When the story of individualism and the story of God are conflated, the gospel ceases to be good news to everyone. For instance, how would you view the American narrative of westward expansion if you were a Native American? Would you tell the story in the same way? Or would you tell a story of deep hurt, dispossession, the eradication of an entire people and their way of life by people who called themselves the children of God? There is a downside to individualism, a dark side.

13

The gospel demands that the Christian should be defined by the story of God more than any rival narrative. The narrative of individualism is one of the most powerful rival gods in American culture. It is espoused and celebrated by many American evangelicals, who seem unaware that it is often antithetical to the Christian story. Becoming a Christian entails switching narratives; moving away from the dominant narratives of the day and toward the narrative we find in the story of God. In our day, the switch is—at least in part—from the narrative of individualism to the narrative of love toward neighbor and enemy alike. Christians should not allow the prevailing wisdom of any given culture to dominate the story of God. If the culture teaches the philosophy of individualism, as ours most certainly does, it becomes necessary for the people of God to resist that philosophy. Not primarily through protests or legislation, but by embodying the great commandment to love God and love people. Only then do we stand as a living witness to the better way.

Jesus is essential to the gospel. Jesus is the gospel. The atonement won by Christ through his blood is essential to the gospel. The life, death, and resurrection of Jesus are all essential to the gospel. But individualism is not. In fact individualism distorts the gospel and renders it powerless in many situations.

THE GOSPEL IN AMSTERDAM

Take this situation for example: Reporter Anthony LoBaido spent time in Amsterdam's red light district in 2001 reporting on the issue of sex trade. Often situated across the street from century-old churches, these modern brothels offer everything under the sun for "sex shoppers." LoBaido tells of walking through one alley and staring into the cold dead eyes of a young prostitute who had been forced into the sex trade. On display in her cage, she was offered to the highest bidder while a group of British tourists walked by and poked fun at her expense. In that dank, dirty alley, after staring into the eyes of the girl in the cage, and hearing the taunting voices, LoBaido simply lost it. He went off on the taunting tourists. "These aren't animals in a zoo," he shouted. "This is a human tragedy. What's wrong with you people? This is somebody's daughter, somebody's sister, somebody's mother," but it made little difference.[1]

1. LoBaido, "In search of Mary Magdalene."

How will the gospel make a difference in the life of the girl in the cage in Amsterdam? To walk up to her and share the four spiritual laws and ask her to pray to accept Christ would be an act of incredible callousness. If the gospel is nothing more than "Jesus died for your sins so you can go to heaven when you die," then it is not good news to her. And if the gospel isn't good news for the girl hanging in a cage in Amsterdam, then it isn't good news at all.[2] The girl in the cage in Amsterdam doesn't need to accept Jesus. She needs Jesus to come get her out of that cage. Our individualized gospel is not enough. It's not enough for her and it's not enough for you or me. The gospel of personal conversion is of no real help to that girl because it's not the whole gospel.

If your temperature is already starting to rise, then this is probably going to boil you over. The gospel isn't meant to address *only* our spiritual slavery to sin, nor is it *only* about how to "get into heaven when you die." The gospel's chief aim is much bigger and more far reaching than that. It concerns our real and present *spiritual, physical, and social slavery* to all kinds of things. It is not merely about the sweet by and by, but also the here and now.

For most of us, however, the individualized gospel of personal conversion is the only tool we've been handed. In fact, over the past few centuries many Western Christians, and nearly all American evangelicals, have slipped into a mode where in our behavior and sometimes our words we say something sort of like this: "Christianity is mostly concerned about your soul. It is about how you can have eternal life. Christianity is about your inner life, your spiritual needs. It's not really that concerned with your body. It's not really concerned about justice. It's not really concerned with the well-being of the planet or physical things. Christianity is about how you can get into heaven when you die—it doesn't bother about the physical needs of this world. This world is going to burn anyway. It's just the place where you decide where you'll spend eternity."

Here's the problem with that. The Bible tells a very different story. *The Bible tells about a God who has always been concerned about all of life*. God is most certainly concerned with your soul and your spiritual needs. But God is also concerned about your physical needs and emotional needs, your financial needs and legal needs, your cultural, relational, intellectual, and educational needs, and so on. And God is concerned about the well-

2. I borrowed this line from Dr. Andy Johnson, who uses a similar example in his lectures on the Gospel of Mark.

being of the planet and about physical things, too. Jesus came not only to save discrete individual souls but to put all of those things into right relationship. God has always been concerned with the whole of creation in all of its interrelatedness.

Christians believe the good news was revealed most perfectly in Jesus Christ, who told us the only way to have all of our needs met was to have faith enough to join with God, as God meets the needs of other people and of the created order as well. Jesus said you will find your life by losing it, and you will lose your life if all you do is try to find it. If all you do is grasp for life, even eternal life, you will lose it all in the end. He told us to seek first the kingdom of God, the place where God reigns and rules as the sovereign of all life. [As we seek first the kingdom of God through Christ, we are changed and transformed into agents of that very transformation—*gospel people* who are being healed and are healing others. God begins to heal our brokenness and we, in turn, learn how to participate in God's mission to heal the brokenness of the world.]

Together we learn how to live as *gospel people* who care for the poor and vulnerable among us. We learn how to love the alien and give them shelter and share our lives with them. We find ways to put an end to corrupt systems, like the ones which allow the girl to suffer in her cage in Amsterdam. We find strength for the day, and we find community and purpose. We find a personal relationship with Christ and with the people of God, too. We find pardon for our sins and the joy of holiness. We learn the most amazing, terrifying, and yet comforting thing we can learn: *God has always been concerned about all of life.* When that happens to us as persons and especially as communities, then all of life begins to come into right relationship with God. That is the good news . . . Thy kingdom come on earth as it is in heaven.

A HELPFUL CONVERSATION PARTNER

I don't know if we realize it, but when we consider heartbreaking issues like sex slavery, or poverty, or racism, or economic injustice, we're actually struggling with the problem of *suffering*. Suffering is everywhere, and it is inescapable. Much of our life's time and energy will be spent trying to avoid, endure, and overcome suffering. One of the things which makes the Christian faith so incredible is this uncanny ability to find the presence of God in the midst suffering. Suffering is not always eliminated by God's presence. In fact we would not want to eliminate all suffering, because it seems to be one of the only sure ways we humans change and grow. Yet, we believe suffering can somehow be redeemed through the presence of God. This is an important component of the good news. Jesus has the ability to redeem our suffering and open up the world to new possibilities of life and peace in the midst of suffering.

I once took a class at seminary in which we were asked to read eight or nine books by the most renowned theologians of the early twentieth century, a century marked by more human suffering than nearly any before it. One of the books I was assigned was by a pastor and theologian named Walter Rauschenbusch. When you are faced with a stack of required reading like that, you really want to know if every book will be worth your time, right? Most of the authors were people I'd heard of: Karl Barth, Rudolf Bultmann, Paul Tillich, Reinhold Niebuhr and the like. I was up for reading them, but seriously, Walter Rauschenbusch? I had never even heard of this guy. However, since it was required reading I figured I'd start with Rauschenbusch's book just to get it out of the way and get on to the good stuff. The book was called *A Theology for the Social Gospel.*

If you travel in contemporary evangelical circles, chances are you haven't heard of Rauschenbusch either, which is sad because he was brilliant. Walter Rauschenbusch was a pastor who served the Second German Baptist Church of New York City from 1886 to 1897. The small church was surrounded by the noisy factories and crowded tenements of the Hell's Kitchen district of New York City. After twelve years of ministry, he wrote a book which made him a national figure, and he became famous nearly overnight. He left Hell's Kitchen to begin a career as a seminary teacher, and continued to write and travel and became known as the father of the "social gospel." Now, although I hadn't heard of Walter Rauschenbusch, I *had* heard of the social gospel. I remember the term because I had always been taught to be wary of it. However, by the time I put the book down, something very profound had changed within me. I had come to discover the truth about the social aspect of the Christian faith.

Part of me wishes I'd never read that book. It totally ruined my game. I knew the moment I read his work that Rauschenbusch had put his finger on the very root of my frustrations regarding the ineffectiveness of my ministries. My old answers to the problem of suffering were exposed as anemic and even cruel. My narrow view of the gospel was expanded and intensified. I was born again . . . again. Before I read Walter Rauschenbusch's book, I thought I had been pretty effective in ministry. I had a decade long run as a Christian artist. I had played and spoken in front of hundreds of thousands of people each year. Our songs were all over Christian radio and our records were in every Christian bookstore. During and after that time I helped to plant three successful churches, all of which thrive to this day. I had written scores of worship songs which are used in worship by churches all over the country. In the evangelical Christian world I was considered accomplished. After I read Rauschenbusch, however, I knew I was failing. I was missing the boat entirely. I was all rocket fuel and no oxygen.

As I looked back on fifteen years of ministry, wondering if anything I had been involved with ever made much of an impact on those who suffer the most, I knew I hadn't had the impact I thought I was having. I also knew I could go to all of the church leadership conferences I wanted and I would not find the help I was looking for. The problem wasn't strategic and the solution wasn't pragmatic. The problem was my vision of the gospel itself. My understanding of the kingdom of God—what I believe God has been up to in this world—was incomplete. It took a man like Walter Rauschenbusch to shake my tree to its roots and open me up to change. He taught me the solution that I was looking for was first and foremost theological in nature. This was a problem of theology and thus the solution must begin there. I refuse to believe the gospel has lost its power. But I cannot escape the reality that the message of personal salvation never seems to get around to changing my neighborhood. Maybe the story of God isn't weak and fruitless, but we just need to understand it better, and tell it in a more compelling way: with our very lives. After all, the best apologetic for the veracity of the gospel is a transformed life.

More than any other pastor and theologian I've read, Walter Rauschenbusch gets the credit for shaking me out of my individualistic gospel coma. His theology isn't perfect. He pushed a lot of ideas in the late nineteenth and early twentieth centuries which would never fly today. Eventually, his hopeful vision of a gospel which is both personal and social in nature became overshadowed and lost to his fellow evangelicals who were whipped into a patriotic fervor by World War I. Still, I have found him to be a very helpful conversation partner in my work. Rauschenbusch was pushing some ideas we need to hear. His writings continue to challenge me, especially as they call into question the theology and practices of most American Evangelical churches I've ever been a part of. I think his writings could make a positive contribution to our faith. Sadly, most evangelicals have never read him or even heard of him. I will draw on his life and theology continually throughout this work.

If you are fairly successful in the evangelical world, I hope to draw out the teachings of Jesus and the theology of Walter Rauschenbusch and let it mess with your head a little bit and maybe help ruin you for an old paradigm of ministry. If you already pursue the call of Scripture toward mercy and justice, chances are you are meeting with resistance, often from those within the church itself. If that is the case, then I hope this study will serve to encourage you and to give you theological rationale for the moves you might be making in your personal life and ministry. If you are just getting serious about your faith and theology, then hopefully this will help give you a head start and save you from some of the anguish I've experienced. Most of all I want to acquaint you with Walter Rauschenbusch and ways in which I think current scholarship vindicates some of his teachings. He was an incredible pastor and theologian who is generally misunderstood and unduly maligned. His life and thought will offer those of us who are committed to a personal faith in Christ, as well as a gospel call to justice and mercy, an effective way to support all we are saying and doing theologically. I hope to evangelize as many people as I can to embrace the good news about God which was proclaimed and enacted by Jesus Christ, and taught so well by Walter Rauschenbusch.

3 Hell's Kitchen

Walter Rauschenbusch is an interesting character. He would have been the seventh generation of university trained German Lutheran pastors from his family; quite a feat for a family who lacked an aristocratic pedigree. However, the string was broken by his father August Rauschenbusch, who, although he was both university trained and a pastor, converted to the Baptist Denomination after he moved to America. Nevertheless, Walter was a seventh generation pastor and a graduate of both the university and seminary.[1] Walter was the first Rauschenbusch born in America. He grew up in Rochester, New York, and was a good student who excelled in every school he attended, including his years at a boarding school in Germany. He graduated at the head of his class from Rochester Seminary and had his pick of appealing ministry assignments. Instead of accepting one of the more prestigious offers, Rauschenbusch chose to move to one of the poorest neighborhoods in all of America. His first and, as it turns out, his only pastorate would be in the slums of New York City. Upon graduation, he would serve as the spiritual leader to the poor German immigrants, most of them industrial workers living in tenements.

Second German Baptist Church was located on the edge of Hell's Kitchen, just a few blocks northwest of the Tenderloin district, where prostitution and gambling thrived. Street gangs and graft pervaded the culture of this community.[2] Today Hell's Kitchen is the trendy Midtown Manhattan home of actors and movie stars. But in Rauschenbusch's day, it was the seedy underbelly of one of the world's largest cities. Nothing in our country today truly approximates what life was like in Hell's Kitchen in the late 1800s. If you've ever seen the Martin Scorsese film *Gangs of New York*, it was set in this same time period in the Five Points area of Manhattan, which was a similar, nearby neighborhood. It's a violent and twisted film.

---

1. Minus, *Walter Rauschenbusch*, 2.
2. Ibid., 49.

20

Yet, if you can wade through the blood and gore, you'll see that Scorsese did a masterful job of drawing out some of the heartbreaking social problems, inhumane working and living conditions, as well as the violence which was commonplace when Walter Rauschenbusch found himself leading that small German Baptist Church. Rauschenbusch believed the gospel must have something to say about these social problems.

Most German immigrants in the city lived in squalor, with multiple families crammed into each tenement building.[3] Hell's Kitchen was a crowded rectangle of apartment buildings and factories which stretched from Fifty-seventh to Thirty-fourth Street, and from Eighth Avenue west to the Hudson River. The Second German Baptist Church was located on West Forty-fifth Street near Tenth Avenue, smack in the middle of Hell's Kitchen. In those days life along Ninth and Tenth Avenues was hard. Typically ten to fifteen people crowded into small, squalid three-room apartments. In addition to the rampant overcrowding, the low wages, crime, disease, unemployment, and hunger made life miserable and often short. Particularly heart-wrenching for Rauschenbusch was the impact on the children. It was reported that 68 percent of the deaths in that time and place were among children aged five and under.[4] Rauschenbusch lived and worked among the people of Hell's Kitchen. He experienced their struggles up close, living each day with the angst of desperate poverty.

What made this even more absurd was that all of this was happening while, just a few blocks up the street, New York's high society was insulated from the suffering lower class. These were the days before labor unions, social security, unemployment benefits, and occupational safety regulations. Safe working conditions and fair wages were not the norm. There were few or no industrial codes and restrictions, nor were there child labor laws. Though some members of the affluent class made meager attempts at charity and relief, the harsh reality was the rich industrial barons and the middle class managers were getting filthy rich on the backs of the immigrant working class of Manhattan. Many of the family fortunes amassed during this period (Rockefeller, Carnegie, Vanderbilt, etc.), survive to this day, bearing witness to the jaded exploitation, abuse, and starvation of those who suffered in Hell's Kitchen less than a mile

3. The Lower East Side Tenement Museum in New York City will give you an up-close look at what life was like for Rauschenbusch and his congregation. Online: http://www.tenement.org/.

4. Rauschenbusch, *Social Gospel*, xiii.

from their opulent homes. Their exploitation of poor working class people became so ugly and transparent that they were given the pejorative nickname, "Robber Barons."

FUELING THE IMAGINATION
BY EXPLOITING THE TENSION

The message Rauschenbusch brought to Hell's Kitchen when he first arrived would be very familiar to the twenty-first century evangelical Christian. He preached about the human journey from sin to salvation. "My idea then," wrote Rauschenbusch "was to save souls in the ordinarily accepted religious sense."[5] Rauschenbusch was a pastor; he preached about repentance and personal salvation with an evangelistic flair. Yet, very early on he began to realize that his message of personal conversion lacked power in his new environment. The poor people of his congregation were already Christians. So were the wealthy barons who treated them like chattel. Personal conversion had little impact upon the miserable social situation of Hell's Kitchen. It wasn't good news to these people who were systematically oppressed by the rich. It wasn't good news to the rich who had grown calloused and indifferent to the tenements and didn't recognize their own culpability. The gospel he was preaching was not making any difference in the world. It was this tension that drove Rauschenbusch to begin to question the individualized gospel and to rediscover the social element of the message of Jesus.

Soon Rauschenbusch began calling his congregation's attention to the biblical rationale for social change. Eventually the poverty of his people began to occupy much of his attention. He was bothered not just by the suffering, but by the apparent lack of feeling with which fellow human beings—and fellow Christians—would oppress one another and take advantage of another's weakness, all the while ignoring their own complicity in the tragic social circumstances.[6] The barons of the Gilded Age seemed content in their ornate homes and churches, while the squalor of the tenements existed nearly undetected, right beneath their noses. Rauschenbusch became convinced he had to help the affluent to see the human toll of their economic practices. His early efforts were much more

5. Minus, *Walter Rauschenbusch*, 98.
6. Ibid., 61.

pragmatic than theological. He simply tried to expose people to the social problems of his neighborhood.

In an article called "Beneath the Glitter," which was published in the *Christian Inquirer* in 1887, Rauschenbusch told the story of a tailor in a clothing house in Manhattan in order to illustrate the situation. The tailor's daughter was dying from consumption (tuberculosis), and had been wasting away for months. The heartbroken father spent his sleepless nights holding his sickly daughter in his arms so she could rest. Night after sleepless night he rocked her and prayed she would recover, but she didn't. As her situation grew more and more grave, he spent every hour possible at her bedside or rocking her quietly in the dark. But on this particular night he couldn't leave work to be with her. His boss forced him to stay and work, threatening to fire him if he left. Rauschenbusch described the tailor, "choking down the sobs and trying to keep the water out of his eyes. Why? Because his little girl is going to die tonight and he can't be there." The daughter dies calling out for her papa to come to her one last time, while the heartbroken tailor works in the shop, fitting the rich people for new suits of clothes.[7] Heartbreaking situations like this were neither fantasy nor fiction; they were commonplace among the people of Rauschenbusch's congregation. As he began to share a common life with those poverty stricken and exploited immigrants, their desperate plight beckoned him to respond. He did so pastorally at first, but soon he began to respond theologically as well. If the tailor could do absolutely nothing about his situation, perhaps Rauschenbusch could. Perhaps his wealthy friends could as well. But if this was going to happen, he would have to develop evangelical theology beyond that which he had previously known. It would take a fuller understanding of the gospel, one which drew people to God and each other. The gospel must respond to the tailor's plight and make a difference.

Rauschenbusch was unique among those living in Hell's Kitchen. He had the ability to navigate two worlds at the same time. He was part of the aristocracy, well educated, well traveled, and highly respected. He rubbed shoulders with the elite and felt comfortable on Manhattan's Upper East Side. It was not hard for him to find publishers who were willing to make his writings known. He was accepted by New York's upper crust. In fact Rauschenbusch and his wife both maintained a longstand-

7. Sharpe, *Walter Rauschenbusch*, 81–82.

ing, friendly relationship with Aura and John D. Rockefeller.[8] Yet day-to-day Rauschenbusch was present to the poor, living and working among them in the tenements. It was this tension between the ultra-rich and the desperately poor, and his ability to navigate both worlds that inspired Rauschenbusch to question his own theology. His experience stretched his individualistic view of the gospel to its breaking point. As he found himself unable to address the deepest needs of his congregation, he began to question his own message. If the gospel he was preaching had no impact on the most pressing issues of the lives of his church members, he was certain the problem could not be the gospel itself, but his understanding of it. He refused to believe the gospel had lost its power and went searching for the missing pieces.

The tension which drove Rauschenbusch to rethink the way he preached the gospel should seem at least a little bit familiar to us. Rauschenbusch had to live with the images of poverty every single day he spent in Hell's Kitchen. You and I live with very similar images. Our computer and television screens pipe them into our homes and offices, and just as Rauschenbusch had to try and reconcile Hell's Kitchen and Madison Avenue, we have to reconcile our suburban American affluence with Sub-Saharan Africa, famine, AIDS, and the reality that two-thirds of the world lives in poverty. As a human race, the problems we face are titanic. There is a lot of darkness in the world. The images of suffering are everywhere, and if we are not acquainted with them it is most certainly because we've worked hard to insulate ourselves from the pain of others. I feel the same tension Rauschenbusch felt and it haunts me every day. It has caused me to question my understanding of the gospel in the same way it did for Rauschenbusch.

In 1907, Rauschenbusch published his first major work, *Christianity and the Social Crisis*. The book called for a Christian response to suffering which was rooted in the Scriptures and the gospel of Jesus Christ. It was a message aimed squarely at the robber barons like the Rockefeller, Carnegie, and Vanderbilt families. He seemed to have written it with at least some level of trepidation. Rauschenbusch wrote his book, sent it to the publisher, and went on a prolonged sabbatical during its release. Privately he wondered if he would even be welcomed back after his sabbatical. Perhaps he would wind up unemployed and ostracized upon his

---

8. Hauerwas, *A Better Hope*, 73.

return. Instead, he came home to discover he had become famous nearly overnight. His book was a huge success in America. He was suddenly thrust into the limelight and began speaking and writing more extensively. Over the course of that decade he would become the leading voice for a new movement which would come to be known as the Social Gospel (a moniker he was never very comfortable with, although he gave in to it). He helped to lead this movement, and to offer a solid theological basis with which to preach a gospel that was not only personal, but corporate as well. This gospel, unlike the individualized gospel, would be good news to those people in Hell's Kitchen and all over the world.

Rauschenbusch was challenging and thought provoking, and in the end I think he was right about the good news Jesus came to enact and proclaim. Now, a century later, many of his ideas seem more relevant than ever. As Rauschenbusch helped the world to see, the gospel of personal salvation is only part of the Christian story. The gospel is personal, to be sure, but it is also social. Although the social aspect of the gospel has been all but lost in contemporary American evangelical theology, any gospel that does not include it is incomplete.

THE TWO GOSPELS

I grew up in a Christian community that revered the Reverend Billy Graham. Whatever you might think about evangelicalism as a movement, you have to admit Graham has been quite incredible over the years. He led his crusade ministry for decades without even a hint of any financial or sexual scandal. He was inexhaustible in both energy and integrity. There's nobody like him. If you listened to the gospel as Billy Graham preached it, as I did many times as a child, it would essentially be about the sin which has caused a breach between *each individual* and God, and how Jesus has bridged that divide. Graham would tell you that if you will accept Christ as Savior, and invite him to live in your heart, you'll be forgiven and can have fellowship with God and assurance of eternal life. In closing, Billy Graham would lead you in the sinner's prayer and ask you to respond by coming forward to the altar. He would make earnest invitations and tell you "the buses will wait." They would sing *Just as I am and waiting not, to rid my soul of one dark blot*, and people would come. It was beautiful. And it changed people's lives forever.

At the same time, I grew up in a community which was somewhat skeptical about Martin Luther King Jr. It was only later on in college that I began to appreciate him as a pastor and as the prophetic leader of the civil rights movement. Whatever you might feel about the civil rights movement in America, you have to respect a man who made the ultimate sacrifice by standing up for those who were suffering the effects of racism. He was brave and courageous in facing down the powers who opposed his efforts. If you listened to the gospel as Dr. King preached it, it would essentially be about the breach between *humanity as a whole* and God. He said the entire nation was out of step with God's ideal, and if America continued down this road God would judge her harshly. He called us to repent of the racism embedded in our cultural systems. Instead of igniting a firestorm of violence he preached the gospel by saying that if we as a country and a people would turn from our wicked ways, God would restore us and heal our land. In closing, Dr. King would ask you to respond by standing in solidarity against segregation. They would sing verse after verse of *We Shall Overcome*, and people would stand together, holding hands. It was beautiful. And it changed people's lives forever.

Billy Graham preached a gospel of personal reconciliation to God saying it was Jesus who had atoned for our sin and would make a way back to right relationship with the creator—rocket fuel. Martin Luther King Jr. preached a gospel of non-violent resistance to evil, saying it was Jesus who wanted to lead all people into right relationship with God, but that will never happen unless we have right relationship with each other—oxygen. Both preached a gospel which was incomplete without the other. Graham needs King and King needs Graham. In fact the two messages are inexorably linked like two sides of the same coin. I believe that if our concept of gospel doesn't include both of these messages, then it is something less than the true gospel found in Scripture, and thus lacks the power to transform the world.

IN THE BEGINNING

Any understanding of the gospel must be grounded in the Scriptures. The story God begins all the way back in Genesis with the account of creation and with the first male and female living in the garden, naive and innocent as children. Any parent of a two-year-old knows that little kids can run naked all over the house without feeling shame. The way they relate to their own bodies is natural and free. It was the same for the first humans. Their relationship with God, with each other, with themselves, and with God's creation was natural, free, and peaceful. They would walk with God in the cool of the day. They had no trouble finding food or peacefully relating to the plants and animals in the garden, and seemed to experience relational harmony between the two of them [I do not think it is oversimplification to say Genesis makes the claim that the first humans were at peace with God, with themselves, with each other, and with all of creation. The whole picture was of harmony and peace.]

Shalom

As the story unfolds, the two fall prey to the lies of the serpent and commit the first transgression. Immediately things begin to change. The way the people of God have chosen to describe this change through the book of Genesis is vitally important. If we do not take into account the nuances of the story, it's very possible we can distort the nature of the problem, and thus the solution to the problem as well.

When God comes looking for Adam and Eve after their rendezvous with the serpent, he finds them hiding. God knew something was up and asked them why they would do such a thing. "I heard the sound of you in the Garden," Adam said, "and I was afraid, because I was naked; and I hid myself."[9] As the conversation unfolds, God questions Adam a little more closely. "Who told you that you were naked? Have you eaten from the tree of which I commanded you not to eat?"[10] Then, in the first ever example of passing the buck, Adam says, "The *woman* whom you gave to be with me, *she* gave me the fruit of the tree and I ate."[11] Can you imagine the look on Eve's face after Adam threw her under the bus like that? So it's no surprise when she tries to do the same thing saying, "The *serpent* tricked me, and I ate."[12] When you are the second one to shift blame it never has the same effect does it? She never even saw it coming.

God teaches Adam and Eve about the consequences of their actions. Each of the consequences discussed in Genesis hold a distinctively *relational* connotation. The results of their actions will impact not only the way they relate to God, but also the way they relate to themselves internally, to each other, and even to the created order. This is extremely im-

9. Genesis 3:10.

10. Genesis 3:11.

11. Genesis 3:12.

12. Genesis 3:13.

portant to keep in mind as we consider this story. The relational fractures which occur as a result of Adam and Eve's sin run in four directions. First, the human relationship with God was fractured—they hid from God. They had never done that before. Second, the human self-relationship was fractured—they saw that they were naked and felt shame for the first time. Third, their relationship to each other was fractured—Adam tried to blame Eve for the debacle. Fourth, their relationship to the created order was fractured—resulting in increased pain in childbirth, and a ground which bore a curse. The story of the fall from the book of Genesis tells of relational damage in *four directions*: between the self and God, the self and the self, the self and other people, and the self and the created order.[13] The gospel story must address and restore all of these fractures for it to be good news.

However, the gospel among evangelicals typically addresses only the fracture of the God-human relationship. The other three parts of the picture are seldom recognized as a vital part of Christ's work on the cross. The Genesis account of the fall serves as a helpful reminder that our own selfishness and sin does not just affect our relationship to *God*, but our relationship to *ourselves*, to *each other*, and to all of *creation*.

Therefore, the gospel message deals not just with our broken relationship with God, but with all of those relationships. We need a savior who can atone for the guilt of sin and repair our relationship with God, for sure. But we also need a savior who can repair all of our brokenness and offer redemption in all four directions—the way we relate to God, to ourselves, to other people and to the world we live in. When we tell the gospel in such a way that the whole story seems to be only about privatized salvation, we reduce the gospel and remove the story of God from its relational context in the Scriptures. The good news of God goes much further than individualized salvation. God's redemption has always been concerned with *all of life*.

---

13. This idea is borrowed from Scot McKnight, and it is explained in much greater detail in his great work, *A Community Called Atonement*, 22.

4 The Gospel among Radical Individualists

There will be opposition to this line of thinking. Individualism has been the air modern culture has breathed since the enlightenment. It is what our forebears taught us yet it stands in profound contrast to the gospel. Making such a claim is to call our very heritage into question. That's a tricky thing to navigate. Rauschenbusch experienced a very similar situation. He believed holding to a way of thinking just because that's what our forebears thought was actually a form of ancestor worship. He once wrote, "Theology needs periodical rejuvenation. Its greatest danger is not mutilation but senility."[1] Senility is what happens when we forget who we are and who we belong to. In some ways our current evangelical theology does suffer from senility. It has forgotten Jesus said it was impossible to love God without loving people. It has forgotten the apostle Paul, who said you could know everything there is to know about God, but if you did not have love, then every time you open your mouth you become like an annoying noise the rest of the world only wants to escape—like a gong or a crashing cymbal. I wonder if the world around us wants to cover their ears when the Christians start talking. If they do, it must be because we have forgotten the biblical mandate to love our neighbors. If we have failed to love our neighbors it is because we have been nurtured in a privatized and individualized Christianity.

Rauschenbusch lived and worked in the early days of industrialization and rapid westward expansion. The persona of the rugged individualist was in full bloom during his time. The great Oklahoma land rush took place in 1889, just as Rauschenbusch was nearing the end of his tenure as a pastor in Hell's Kitchen. To the rugged individualist, there had hardly ever been a better time or better place to live than this time in America. Yet, since his congregation was comprised of the immigrants who worked in the factories and foundries, Rauschenbusch saw the dark

1. Rauschenbusch, *Social Gospel*, 12.

side of American individualism; the side which could exploit young children to the point of death in the factories and sweat shops. We like to think of American Individualism as this inner drive pushing the individual to achieve greatness. But we seldom stop and consider how it can, and did, become a serious impediment to our sense of the common good.

Rauschenbusch believed individualism was a real problem when it came to embracing the true gospel, because the true gospel involves a turning to neighbor in love as well. Do you remember how Jesus responded to the question concerning the greatest of the commandments? He emphasized two: love God, love your neighbor. The two are inseparable. Any robust conception of the gospel must take into account Jesus's teaching about loving God and neighbor. Moreover, Jesus seemed to assume any sincere response to the gospel would have to follow suit. Responding to Jesus involves a turning away from individualism and a turning toward our fellow human beings in love. If the gospel we preach, teach, and follow does not make this demand upon our lives—that we should renounce our radical individualism and embrace to call to love our neighbor—then it is not the same gospel we find in the New Testament. Any sort of personal salvation that does not involve this view is something very different than Jesus envisioned. Rauschenbusch taught that salvation should involve a conversion from individualism to personhood, or what he called the "socializing of the soul." By this I believe he meant a turning away from focus on the individual with their desires, wants, and needs, toward the whole of a society or social group and a focus on peaceful and "right" relating across the whole group. When Rauschenbusch made this move, he paved the way for many subsequent theologians and philosophers who began to deconstruct individualism in favor of personhood.

Throughout *A Theology for the Social Gospel*, Rauschenbusch decries the individualism of his time. One of the major recurring themes in the book is what he called, "an attempt to overcome the exaggerated individualism into which Protestantism was thrust by the violent reactions of the Reformation."[2] Rauschenbusch often linked this blind allegiance to individualism with the reactionary impulse of the Protestant Reformation; a reaction against the autonomy of the Roman Catholic Church. As the reformers fought to counter the church's absolute power, it was natural that they would "deny every claim by which the enemy could brace its

2. Ibid., 123.

authority."³ Much of the corruption evident in the Catholic Church of that era certainly needed reforming. Yet Rauschenbusch rightly asserts that it may have gone too far. "The result of this great polemical reaction against the [Roman Catholic] Church was a system of religious individualism in which the social forces of salvation were slighted, and God and the individual were almost the only realities in sight."⁴ This was an amazing observation for his time. In the Protestant Reformation, the autonomy of the church was merely replaced with the autonomy of the individual. The problem Rauschenbusch sought to address was how to get people to recognize the essential nature of human solidarity and community over and against the ubiquitous assertion of individual autonomy.

Luckily, in the years since Rauschenbusch did his work, much has transpired in this arena. Theologians and philosophers have made great strides toward demystifying the individual. In so doing, I believe Rauschenbusch's instincts have been vindicated. What follows in this chapter is an attempt to summarize the argument against radical individualism from those who came after Rauschenbusch and who carry on the project to which he devoted his life.

SEVEN YEARS IN TIBET

The individual, as it is commonly understood in our culture, is a myth. It is a distortion of reality which has little to do with the Jewish or the Christian understanding of personhood. In our faith, we believe the person is constituted, first and foremost, *in community*. This has been the argument advanced by many of our contemporary theologians. It is also beginning to find its way into art and film.

Seven Years in Tibet is the true story of the Austrian adventurist Heinrich Harrer, who is played by Brad Pitt. Heinrich Harrer was a national hero to the people of Austria. He was a world champion alpine skier, a famous mountain climber, and a celebrity of epic proportion for his time. He was talented and ambitious, but as it is with many people of that type, it seems Harrer was not exactly easy to get along with. Truth be told, he was this completely self-absorbed and arrogant man who seemed to leave a trail of broken relationships in his wake. In 1939, Harrer and a team of climbers set out to climb Nanga Parbat in the Himalayas. After

3. Ibid.
4. Ibid.

failing to reach the summit, the climbers returned to their base camp only to discover that Germany had invaded Poland and World War II had begun. Harrer's entire team was behind enemy lines where they were captured and held in India by the British. Soon after that, he and a few other climbers escaped their internment camp and crossed over into Tibet in an attempt to wait out the war there.

Tibetan culture could not have been more different from Austrian culture. Harrer quickly learned the things that mattered in Germany and Austria didn't matter at all in Tibet. At home, the only way he knew to distinguish himself was by winning gold medals and climbing mountains— pursuing fame and celebrity through individual achievement. In Tibet these things were considered vices. There's a scene in the movie where he and his best friend are both trying to impress a beautiful Tibetan girl. They run across several pairs of ice skates in a flea market and decide to try them out together. Harrer attempts to win the girl's affections by showing off, skating fast, and doing these lame figure skating moves; it's actually pretty funny. His friend attempts to win her affections by helping her to learn to skate and patiently attending to her. Harrer chooses the path of individual achievement and distinction while his friend chooses the path of humility and service. In the end, it is Harrer's humble friend who wins the affections of the Tibetan girl.

The movie shows a brief exchange where the girl explains to Harrer that her culture doesn't value individual achievement, being first, winning, or holding one's self above others. They have a very different concept of virtue. Tibetans value humility, innocence, tranquility, peace, harmony, etc. They embrace the gradual letting go of one's ego. Thus they would never openly show off or aspire to win competitions and hold themselves up as better than their fellow human beings. It would be counter-productive. People would actually think less of them, not more. They valued oneness and solidarity above individualism and achievement. *Seven Years in Tibet* is really a movie about Heinrich Harrer's personal transformation from one symbolic world to another. Slowly but surely over the course of the story, the old marks of success and virtue and a life well lived begin to fall away and new ones grow in their place. The old symbols of success are exposed as the symbols of selfishness and folly. By the end of the movie, Harrer is a completely different person.

I think the story of Heinrich Harrer's relationship with the people of Tibet teaches us a very important reality concerning the human condition. The culture in which we live shapes and forms us. Our community teaches us what to value and what to pursue with our lives. The culture gives us lenses through which we view the entire world. Those lenses have great authority over the people who live within a given culture. In particular, our American culture has given us lenses that are extremely individualistic, not unlike the culture of Austria or any other Western country. We are a culture consumed with individual rights, individual freedoms, and individual achievement. The individual reigns supreme in our culture, often even above the common good. Is it any wonder the gospel we tell only concerns how the individual can find salvation and eternal life?

The gospel Jesus preached was nothing less than a completely new set of lenses through which to view the world. Jesus had a very different way to view reality—especially personhood—and he gave new symbols for what it means to have an abundant life.

NEW LENSES

In the Sermon on the Mount Jesus redefined the symbols of the good life for his followers. He taught them about the way he viewed the world, and gave them a chance to wear new lenses. As he spoke, Jesus ran through a litany of the people who will be blessed in the kingdom of God. If you take these words seriously, you have to admit he was championing all the wrong people. The poor in spirit, the mourners, the meek, the merciful, the pure in heart, and the peacemakers—they were the ones he cited. Think of how that must have sounded to his first listeners. They lived in a rough and violent world. If someone broke into your house you couldn't just call the police and expect them to come to your defense. You had to grab your club and defend yourself, your family, and your property. To them it would have sounded like Jesus was saying, "Blessed are the weenies." Jesus's advice would have seemed completely impractical, and perhaps even a little bit silly. In our dog-eat-dog world Jesus's teaching seems equally impractical.

I think Jesus anticipated this response when he turned to a very effective rhetorical device, "You've heard it said . . . but I say." You've heard it said don't murder, but I say even anger toward a brother or sister is the same as murder. You've heard it said don't commit adultery, but I say lusting in your heart is the same thing. You've heard it said an eye for an eye, but I say turn the other cheek. You've heard it said love your neighbor and hate your enemy, but I say love your enemies and pray for those who persecute you. You've heard it said you should view the world one way, but I say you should view it a completely different way. You have heard it said the kingdom of God will come one way, but I say it will come by a completely different way. You have these old lenses over your eyes, but I say it is possible to receive new lenses, and thus to see the world in a different way, to receive a vision of the kingdom of God. Jesus completely redefined the symbols of virtue for his followers, and each time he did, the movement he described was toward other people in solidarity, love, and forgiveness. This is the way of the kingdom. We need to discard the lenses of individualism and begin to see the world through the eyes of Christ.

The truth is, the journey Jesus calls each of us to is quite analogous to the journey Heinrich Harrer took in Tibet: away from individualism and self-assertion, and toward love of God and neighbor. The Western world often feels it has a corner on the wisdom market. Eastern people have a less difficult time with the movement away from individualism for obvious reasons. The East did not experience the Enlightenment period, nor were they affected by the Reformation in the same way as the West. Rationalism never held sway in Eastern culture. Before we dismiss all Eastern religion as wrong, we should be reminded that Jesus lived in the East, and Second Temple Judaism was an Eastern religion. Jesus was not a rationalist, nor was he a fan of radical individualism, and his teaching was much more Eastern than Western.

Jesus taught that love toward our fellow human beings—even our enemies—is the path to God. This, to Jesus, was not some ancillary teaching which should be tacked onto the gospel and called something like discipleship or holiness. This is the gospel he preached. You cannot love God if you do not love your neighbor. This is how we see God. This is how we are blessed. This is how we inherit the earth. This is the good news.

More than anything else, what keeps us from experiencing Jesus's vision of the kingdom of God, what keeps us from knowing redemption in all four directions, is this lens of American individualism. It is the most widely embraced, uncritically accepted, yet damaging and humanly debasing myth in Western society. Individualism tells us many things about ourselves which turn out to be lies and half-truths. In order to fully embrace the message of Jesus, Christians must begin to deconstruct the god of individualism and embrace a more relational idea of personhood.

A RELATIONAL VIEW OF PERSONHOOD

It is important to distinguish the difference between the concept of the individual and the concept of the person. Let me be clear about the way I will use those two terms. The *individual* is an idea which refers to a distinct entity that is capable of independent existence. The *person* refers to a human being, as opposed to an animal or a thing, who is defined by their association to the larger group of people. Individuality connotes autonomy while personhood connotes belonging. Conversion to Christ is really about belonging. It's about leaving behind our individual rights and freedoms and becoming a slave to Christ. It's about leaving behind our obsessive need to distinguish ourselves so that we can become a part of the people of God—that's true freedom. This requires a conversion from false individualism to true personhood; from self-referential existence to a way of being which is necessarily constituted in and through relationship. Personhood—and thus salvation—requires us to have a relational view of human agency. The twenty-five cent word for this is *ontology*, or the nature of "being." Human ontology is relationally or socially construed. What makes us human is our participation in humanity.

The classic philosophical statement of this view can be found in G.H. Mead's *Mind, Self, and Society*. The argument contained in Mead's book, which was published in 1934, is compelling. The point I want to accentuate here is that the human awareness of "the self" naturally comes through an experience of "the other." The preeminent American theologian Stanley Hauerwas sums up Mead's argument by saying, "The self is fundamentally social. We are not individuals who come into contact with others and then decide our various levels of social involvement. Our individuality is possible only because we are first of all social beings. I know who I am only in relation to others, and, indeed, who I am is a relation with others. The 'self' names not a thing, but a relation."[5]

This is the relational view of personhood. What defines me as a person is not my individuality or uniqueness, but my essential connectedness to other people. The only way I can tell who I am as a person—or discern that I exist at all—is in relationship to other people and to God. Personal existence is necessarily social. The social relationship temporally and logically precedes any awareness of our own existence. In other words, if I was the only thing in existence, it would not be possible for me

5. Berkman and Cartwright, *Hauerwas Reader*, 372.

to even discern my own existence. This is, of course, an important part of the Genesis story and one of the most basic building blocks of the story of God. God saw that it was not good for Adam to be alone, so God created other humans in order that Adam might live in community and know who he was. The only way Adam could be fully human as God intended him to be was if he was a person in community.

William T. Cavanaugh rightly asserts another connection to the Genesis story. He says, "The effect of sin is the very creation of individuals as such, that is, the creation of an ontological distinction between individual and group."[6] Individualism is a sort of cult-of-the-self which is always a direct result of selfishness. It is not a virtue to be touted, nor is it a God-given part of what it means to be human. It is a distortion of personhood, a distortion of God's good creation. To give in to the myth of individualism is to give in to the power of sin over all of humankind.

Although the self is constituted in relationship, the distinct identity and personhood of every human being is still very important. Every person is unique. Yet according to the great Eastern Orthodox theologian John Zizioulas, *each person's uniqueness is not rooted in our individuality, but in our community*. Zizioulas grew up in the East. Thus, he is not captivated by the individualism of the West. He argues that a person's uniqueness comes through participation in community. As we turn to one another in love, each person recognizing the worth and value of the other, we become irreducible, unrepeatable, and unique; which is to say we truly become persons.[7] Without community we can never be fully human. Community is woven into our very being. We are born into the world as biologically dependent organisms. There's no such thing as an individualistic baby, they must be nurtured in community or they will die. We need community in order to reproduce. There is no such thing as asexual human reproduction. Without community, the human race would cease to exist. Human ontology—our very being—is predicated upon community. Community comes first.

Zizioulas builds this argument from the church fathers and the Scriptures, not from Platonic philosophy. The church fathers employed the concept of personhood as a way to describe the concept of the Trinity—three persons, one essence. God exists as community. Zizioulas

6. Smith, *Introducing Radical Orthodoxy*, 235.

7. Zizioulas, *Being as Communion*, 39–49.

says our uniqueness as human persons is not rooted in what we can achieve as individuals, but in our relationship to other people who are distinct from us.

Just stop and consider the words of Hauerwas, Zizioulas, and Cavanaugh in light of our American culture. The ontological distinction between the individual and the group is a huge part of the American narrative. We try to achieve our uniqueness instead of receiving it from the community to which we belong. Our society seems possessed by this insatiable thirst to distinguish ourselves from other people. Over time this has morphed into a full-blown culture of fame. Fame is now a virtue in our society, and people will do nearly anything to stand apart from the crowd. Andy Worhol predicted our fifteen minutes of fame; I wonder if he knew that the fifteen minutes would be virtually meaningless and unfulfilling.

One of the more notorious examples of this in recent history was the ill-fated hoax of the Balloon Boy, Falcon Heene. In 2010, the Heene family released a flying-saucer-shaped balloon filled with helium into the air from their home in Ft. Collins, Colorado, then alerted the media that they believed their six-year-old son Falcon was in the balloon. It scared the be-jeebers out of the entire country who watched it live on MSNBC, et al. In the end, it turned out to be a hoax planned by the family that was only exposed when Falcon couldn't keep his story straight in front of the cameras. Apparently the motivation behind their plan was nothing more than a desire to make their family more marketable; to distinguish themselves from other people. It worked, too. Yet, this sense of individuality actually runs in direct opposition to the message of Jesus. Just imagine Jesus saying, "Blessed are the winners of American Idol for they shall see God. Blessed are the first round draft picks, for they will inherit the earth." It's absurd isn't it? Why is it absurd? *Because we cannot achieve our uniqueness, it is given to us by God.* So God sets the terms and God's terms are: you will only experience what it means to be fully human as you participate in the human community. You will never experience what it means to be fully human by expressing your individuality at the expense of the group. That is a dehumanizing move which is ultimately self-defeating.

This is exactly the Apostle Paul's view of the community of Christians he addresses in 1 Corinthians 12. He says the church is the body, and the body has many parts; a hand, a foot, a thumb, an eye, etc. A hand is not a person, nor is a foot or an eye a person. This is the biblical analogy of personhood. Just as a hand is worthless without the body, so the individual is worthless without an integral association to the group. The hand finds its proper value in relation to the body as a whole. The individual finds its proper value in relation to humanity as a whole.

Every person is really a "person in relation to other people," because we are indissolubly connected to one another. Our distinctiveness and worth as human persons isn't something we "do" by winning American Idol, becoming a pro athlete, getting our faces on the front page, or making a ton of money. Our distinctiveness isn't something we can accomplish, it is given to us by God, and it is discovered and celebrated within the context of community. *Community is constitutive of being* and not the other way around. Our "being," human ontology, our very existence as human beings is given to us by God through community. We receive it from God and from the people whom God has created.

This is part of why the gospel cannot be rightly communicated through individualistic categories of thought. Zizioulas once wrote that Christian community, and thus true being, is formed "through a radical conversion from individualism to personhood in baptism." [8] I think he's right. Following after Jesus involves a conversion from individualism to personhood. This, in fact, is a very healthy way to view our own baptism. Baptism should actually be seen as a renunciation of individualism (or any rival god for that matter), as we join with the people of God and become fully human persons. In the evangelical tradition, many churches practice either infant baptism or adult baptism. Both forms of this sacrament are meant to symbolize the person as a new reality constituted by God. The person dies to the old way of being which is marked by selfishness and individuality, and they enjoin a whole new way of being human marked by their identity which is found in and through the community. They renounce their citizenship in the kingdom of the world (or the parents renounce it symbolically for them), and the people of God declare that they are citizens of the kingdom community. Having jettisoned the concept of radical individualism as the source of our uniqueness, we can be converted to true personhood. After this conversion we can begin to reconsider how personal salvation and corporate salvation—Billy Graham and Martin Luther King Jr.—must fit together as one unified gospel message.

8. Ibid., 113.

5 Created in the Image to Be an Image

The temptation at this point is to launch straight away into a doctrine of corporate sin and salvation, and we will get to that shortly. However, there is an important fundamental point we have to consider first. It has been my experience that most Protestant theologies of sin begin with the story of the fall of Adam and Eve and work from there. This has typically been the Western tack. I think we need a different approach, one more like that of the Eastern church, and Walter Rauschenbusch. I believe we must begin not with the story of the fall, but with the story of creation. Any consideration of how we fall short must start first with an idea of what we are falling short from. What is God's purpose for human beings? What is our *telos*, our reason for existence? What are we supposed to do and be? These are the first questions that must be explored. By starting here, we can attempt to understand the nature of human sinfulness in light of God's original intentions for humanity.

To answer these important questions we can begin by considering who God is, or the nature of God. Rauschenbusch insightfully considers the nature of God in relation to the social gospel. He notes that any "conception of God held by a social group is a social product. Even if it originated in the mind of a solitary thinker or prophet, as soon as it becomes the property of a social group, it takes on the qualities of that group."[1] Rauschenbusch recognized that to experience God's self-revelation, consider it, refine it, interact with it over time, and then to preserve and teach that experience to consecutive generations over several millennia is an incredible social achievement. This is not a reality to be embarrassed of, nor should we attempt to cover it over with religious zeal-spouting—"God said it, I believe it, that settles it!" The fact that the very concept of God is transmitted and enhanced over time via culture is a great gift to humanity that should be celebrated. If this were not the case, then our awareness of

1. Rauschenbusch, *Social Gospel*, 167.

God would be significantly diminished. Rauschenbusch wrote, "If every individual had to work out his idea of God on the basis of his own experiences and intuitions only, it would be a groping quest, and most of us would see only the occasional flitting of a distant light. By the end of our life we might have arrived at the stage of voodooism or necromancy."[2] Rauschenbusch said to enter into a discussion of the nature of God is "like entering a public park or a public gallery of art and sharing in the common wealth."[3] Our concept of God is a socially mediated thing. We should be thankful for this. It means that we have grown—that God's self-revelation does not return to God void but has an affect on societies and cultures.

This may create tension for those of us who grew up learning that the only way to understand anything about God is to read the Bible. But the Bible is not self-explanatory. Just as the Ethiopian eunuch needed Philip to help him understand what he was reading, we need help as well. No one can read the Bible apart from community. For one thing it is a written document. You cannot read it unless you've been taught how to read. One has to know the language, and language is socially and culturally mediated. You have to be taught the meaning of words by someone else before you can read them. No one is born with the ability to read and understand words. For another thing, the Bible was written in languages hardly any of us can read. It has to be translated into a language which we can understand. This means as soon as we pick up an English translation, we are reading a text which has been mediated by someone else. Lastly, the Bible was never intended to be read apart from community. For the first fifteen hundred years of the Bible's existence, until the invention of the printing press, it was read privately only in very rare cases. Our ability to read comes from community, as does the Bible itself. People love to point to the case of the addict who grabs the Gideon's Bible from the hotel room and comes to faith in Christ as an individualistic event. But, who taught him to read? Who put the Bible there? Who translated it into English? Who authored it? Who decided what writings would be included and not included in the canon? Much of what we know about God has come to us through community and has been mediated by that community under the guidance of the Spirit.

2. Ibid., 168.

3. Ibid.

This underlying belief led Rauschenbusch to celebrate the incarnation as the moment when our concept of God became engaged in its most radical stage of development. Rauschenbusch believed that since our conceptions of God are socially mediated, they will always be tainted with the philosophies and ideals of any given society. In a world where might makes right, theological descriptions of God are likely to follow suit. Rauschenbusch's consistent indictment of government and church alike was to call it *despotism* (the autocratic system of rule). A despotic government will fund theologians who come up with a despotic conception of God and the universe. But the incarnation ruined that project forever. Rauschenbusch wrote, "When [Jesus] took God by the hand and called him 'our Father,' he democratized the conception of God. He disconnected the idea from the coercive and predatory State, and transferred it to the realm of family life, the chief social embodiment of solidarity and love."[4] No longer could we view God as distant and tyrannical. God had entered in. Those who persist in autocratic or individualistic views of God run the risk of denying the importance of the incarnation and perpetuating the belief in a despotic God. Rauschenbusch went so far as to say, "We have classified theology as Greek and Latin, as Catholic and Protestant. It is time to classify it as despotic and democratic. From a Christian point of view that is a more decisive distinction."[5]

Rauschenbusch never came out with a systematic explanation of his doctrine of God. He did not develop his idea of the democratization of God into a full blown Social Trinity. But in the century following his life, more work was done along these lines. What follows is an attempt to note where some of the current thinking in regard to the image of God might help us to begin to consider the specific doctrine of sin from a social point of view.

THE TRINITY AS A MODEL FOR PERSONHOOD

From the first generation of Christ followers to present day, God has been described via the use of a concept called Trinity. In the Western church we generally think about the Trinity by starting with a solitary concept of God, and then we ask how this one God can be three distinct persons. Our driving question has been, "How can this one God be three?" With

4. Ibid., 175.

5. Ibid.

such emphasis always on the oneness of God, it is not surprising that the resulting forms of theology should be individualistic. This is the image we have of God and thus the image we have of ourselves. In the Eastern church, it has been the other way around. They begin with the three and then ask, "How can this three be one?" The resulting forms and structures of theology in the Eastern church seem to be more relational and balanced, largely focused on the communal nature of God's being. This different emphasis has resulted in some insights and appreciations which seem to be ignored by the Western church. We're too often content to persist with individualistic modes of Christianity.

Our Orthodox brothers and sisters help us realize that the Triune God exists eternally as a community. The Father, Son, and Holy Spirit are distinct persons, but they are of one essence. Father, Son, and Spirit enjoy a life of mutual love. This love which flows between the three persons of the Trinity never can never be exhausted; it will go on forever. The Trinity can be called a plurality-in-oneness: three distinct persons inseparably joined by this never ending flow of ecstatic love. Father loving Spirit and Son, Spirit loving Son and Father, Son loving Father and Spirit—an endless community of love. *The very life of God is a community of love.*

We who are created in God's image have a similar kind of existence. Understanding this helps us to answer the questions we have about God's purpose for human beings. What are we supposed to do and be? In essence, we are supposed to image the Holy Trinity, the God in whom we live, and move, and have our being. Just as God exists as three persons and one essence, humanity should exist as a communal entity made of many persons. In fact, all of creation is a result of the eternal love that exists between the Father, Son, and Spirit. God's love found its expression in the creation of the cosmos. The earth we inhabit is nested in this cosmos, which exists as the love child of the Trinity. This is what it means to be created in the image of God: we are all distinct persons, but we share one human essence as well. It also means that our very lives are conceived and given to us within the context of community. We come from community and we are meant for community.

This relational view of the image of God finds great support within the early chapters of Genesis. Here we find God's vision for human vocation. First, the Triune God says, "Let us make humankind in our image, according to our likeness; and let them have dominion."[6] That's how it starts. Humanity comes from the community of the God-head, and is endowed with some sort of privileged status over the rest of creation. Humans are to have a limited amount of power to rule creation as God's representative creatures. Second, God says, "Be fruitful and multiply, and fill the earth and subdue it."[7] To be fruitful and multiply connotes a co-creative function. We've been created with the potential to be co-creators with God. We can make stuff. We can even make more people. It seems to be God's desire that humanity should take this creative power everywhere we can go. We must fill the earth and bring it under our dominion. Third, we are told in the next chapter God has put humans in the garden "to till it and keep it."[8] Our vocation isn't just to rule over creation, but to keep it and care for it. We are stewards of creation. We should work with the earth and help it to bear the fruit that sustains life. We should not exploit the earth and its resources, but we should protect it and be its keeper. According to Genesis our vocation as human beings is threefold: we are to be fruitful and multiply; we are to fill the earth and subdue it by exercising dominion over it; we are to till the earth and keep it. These three concepts constitute the seedbed for a biblical view of human vocation.

When we pursue this vocation faithfully both as persons, and as a community, we will begin to *image* God to all creation. This concept of imaging God may not be intuitive to us. To say that humans were meant to image God is one of the best ways to speak in overarching terms about human vocation. We are made in the image of God and we are meant to be image bearing creatures. The Greek word for "image" is the word *eikon* ("icon"). The terms can be used interchangeably. In a discussion about what it means to be a human person, the metaphor of the icon is essential. Sadly, for most evangelicals this is a foreign concept. Therefore, in order to begin to understand human vocation we must first understand the concept of the *icon* a little better.

ICON

In the early days of the Second Gulf War, the United States military forces were pressing into the heart of Baghdad, and the imbedded reporters

6. Genesis 1:26.

7. Genesis 1:28.

8. Genesis 2:15.

were transmitting images back to America constantly. As the troops entered Baghdad, everywhere they went they showed these huge icons of Saddam Hussein. In the market, there would be an icon of Saddam holding bread—he was the feeder of the nation. In the schools there would be an icon of Saddam holding the books—he was the keeper of all knowledge. In the town square there would be an icon of Saddam with a rifle—he was the protector of the people. The icon of Saddam Hussein was always present in Iraqi society so that everyone would always know who was in control and who was responsible for all that they had. Saddam could not be present everywhere, but his icon could be in nearly every environment, witnessing to his power and control. This is the role of the icon. The icon points past the object which is seen to the greater reality which stands behind it. Perhaps this is why the very first thing many Iraqi people did after the fall of Baghdad was to remove the statues and icons of Saddam from public squares, schools, and even their homes. He no longer ruled and so his icon meant nothing.

In ancient Rome it was the icon of the Emperor. In cold war China it was the icon of Chairman Mao. In America the icon is not a person but a thing. The quintessential American icon is the flag. It represents the rule of law and the reign of a people who must consent to be governed. The American flag is present in nearly every environment, bearing witness to the sovereign rule of the people. The flag is an icon. *The purpose of an icon is to make the ruler present in every situation.*

Human beings were created to be the icons of the triune God—to make our ruler present in every situation. The best way I know how to say it is this: Our vocation as human beings is to organize our common life together in such a way that we image God to all creation and bear witness to the in-breaking kingdom of God, so that when all of creation looks at us and sees the way we live together—not just as individuals—it will see past us to the greater reality that is the reign and rule of God. This vision for human vocation should have a powerful impact on the way we view God's purpose for our lives. God's vision for human vocation must be the basis from which we begin to talk about human sinfulness or salvation, so the way we organize our common life together matters a great deal. Christianity is not primarily about discrete individuals having a particular set of correct and orthodox beliefs about God which results in eternal life. The Christian faith is a way of being; a way of relating to God, ourselves, other humans, and all of creation. It is not a belief system.

It is not a religion. It is a way of being fully human as humanity was always intended by God.

It is interesting to consider the way the Scriptures bear this idea out. For our purposes here we can stick with the Genesis story. There seem to be several major starting or re-starting points that mark God's relationship to humanity in the book of Genesis. Each plays an important role in our understanding of human vocation. The first is the creation narrative from Genesis 1-3. God speaks the cosmos into creation and gives human beings their vocation: "be fruitful and multiply."[9] Although humans fail to live up to their calling, the calling continues just the same. We can see proof of this as we read on in Genesis. The second major point is the re-starting of the human project we find after the flood in the story of Noah. Here God destroys almost everything and starts over again. When Noah and his family come out of the ark God reminds them of their vocation using the same exact words he used with Adam and Eve: "be fruitful and multiply."[10] The third is when God calls Abraham. He is told to leave his home and God will multiply his family. They will be like the stars. Abraham will be blessed by God so that he can be a blessing to all the people of the world.[11] Here the wording is different, but the concept is the same: "be fruitful and multiply and image me wherever you go." The fourth is when God renames Jacob, calling him Israel and establishing a people by the same name who will become the people of God. Once again God recites the human vocation using those same words: "be fruitful and multiply."[12] At each of these pivotal points in the story of God, the command to be fruitful and multiply is repeated. Each time it reaches back to God's plan for the human vocation and the whole complex of meanings found in Genesis 1 and 2. God is a plurality in oneness, a community of out-flowing love; and human beings are created in that image. We were given a vocation—be fruitful, multiply, fill the earth, subdue it, till it, keep it—to organize our common life together in such a way that we image the reign and rule of God to all of creation. To do anything else is to fail to be fully human. For, as John of Kronstadt was said to be fond of saying to

9. Genesis 1:26; 2:15.

10. Genesis 9:1, 7.

11. Genesis 12.

12. Genesis 35:11.

the drunk Russians as he picked them out of the gutters, "This is beneath your dignity. You were meant to house the fullness of God."

SIN AS FAILURE TO IMAGE GOD

The image of God and the corporate aspect of sin are linked via the concepts of the Trinity and human vocation. The very word "sin" can be used may ways. Here I use sin as a word or a concept in order to describe the most basic problem which is universal to the human experience: humanity's failure to be faithful to our original human vocation. Sin is a failure to organize our common life together in such a way that we image God to all creation. Sin is a failure to be fruitful and multiply, to fill the earth and keep it, and to exercise loving dominion over it—a failure to be fully human as human is meant to be. Typically the way the Scriptures describe this is that we cease to image God and begin to image ourselves. Instead of bearing God's image we make idols of ourselves and begin to worship created things. Our most basic understanding of sin must be a corporate failure of vocation; a way of being less than fully human, or what Mark Biddle calls, "inauthentic existence."[13]

Yet this is not how we generally talk about sin. Sin is usually viewed individualistically. Typical individualistic notions of sin adopt what Biddle describes as a "sin as crime" metaphor where sin is viewed as a crime that is committed against God.[14] It is something perpetrated by an individual which requires some sort of punishment in order for the justice of God to be upheld. Thus the remedy for sin will be construed in individualistic categories, i.e., Jesus as the perfect sinless individual takes the place of the imperfect sinful individual and takes the punishment for the crime. Biddle rightly asserts that this individualization of sin is a classic example of trying to take a narrative like the Genesis account of the fall and convert it into a system. Narratives, by their very nature, resist that sort of systematization. Perfect, tight systems typically involve some sort of dangerous distortion.

The way to avoid the individualistic distortion of the Scriptures is to do our very best to view the story as a whole. How were we created and what were we created for? How have we failed to be and do those things? These are the questions we should ask when it comes to considering the

13. Biddle, *Missing the Mark*, xvii.

14. Ibid., viii–xvi.

concept of sin. If the goal of God's human project is a particular kind of common life, then sin is the failure to engender that vision in the way we live. Sin is most certainly something we hold in common. At its most basic level, sin is a communal phenomenon. Individual transgressions are certainly worthy of being called "sin" but they do not come close to explaining the power of sin in all of its complexities and the ways in which is has been woven into systems and situations of our culture.

Tucked neatly in between the stories of Noah and the call of Abraham, we find the curious account of the Tower of Babel. This is a classic Genesis example of corporate sin. Here we find a society organizing their common life together in such a way that they image *themselves* to all of creation. "Come, let us build ourselves a city," they said, "with a tower that reaches to the heavens, so that we may make a name for ourselves and not be scattered over the face of the earth."[15] It's striking how closely the language used in this story of corporate sin resembles the language used for basic human vocation. At Babel, the community's agenda was to build a tower and make a name for themselves. They moved from being icons to being idol makers; from a people who bear the image of God to a people set on imaging themselves. The story also contains a specific reference to their refusal to fill the earth. The reason for building the city is at least in part, *so they will not be scattered,* in direct defiance of God's original instructions. The people refuse to pursue their God-given vocation to fill the earth.

The account of Babel is a story of a people who have refused to live up to the most basic human vocation, be fruitful and multiply, and be God's image bearing creatures throughout the earth. Immediately following this refusal, God calls Abraham and begins to form a people who will actually bear his image to the world. God's call to Abraham and God's subsequent plans and dreams for the people of Israel directly follow the Noah story and Babel, both of which are examples of corporate sinfulness. *God moves not merely in response to individual sins and transgressions, but to corporate sin.* When God scatters them and frustrates their language at Babel, it is not a random act of judgment or punishment. It is evidence of God's resolve that the human vocation must go on. Humans must fulfill their iconic function throughout all of creation. God will not accept the alternative. Humans should live everywhere in creation, to enhance it,

15. Genesis 11:4.

order it, and organize it in a way that gives glory to God—that icons God. From this early point in Genesis we can tell sin must be viewed not as merely personal, but as a corporate thing as well. The stories of Noah and Babel clearly have corporate sinfulness in view. God's response to each is to find a way to move humans without compromise toward the fulfillment of their vocation.

All throughout the Scriptures we are told about the God who is trying to find a people who will image God to all of creation. God begins with the patriarchs: Abraham, Isaac, Jacob, and his sons, especially Joseph. When the project was derailed in Egypt, God sent the prophet Moses to get it back on track. Yet, even after God's mighty actions, his people still would not fully embrace their vocation. The judges and the kings of Israel were attempts to help Israel to organize their lives and embrace their iconic calling. The prophets called the people to return to their vocation, but they never did. Throughout each era and epic in the story of the people of God, their failure was a corporate failure; their sinfulness was a corporate sinfulness. When all of God's attempts to help humanity organize their common life in such a way to give glory to God and image God to all creation had failed, God finally resolved to come and do it himself. This is the true meaning of the incarnation of God in Christ. God comes to break the powers that keep us from being fully human as human was meant from the very beginning. Jesus gets it done where the children of Israel cannot. Our individualistic notions of sin often tend to shrink the mission of Jesus into a sort of stealth suicide mission. Only a corporate view of sin can help us to see that Jesus's mission is consistent with the mission of God we find throughout the story of God: the restoration of all the community of creation to its right relationship to God and to itself.

6 A Serious and Humble Sense of Sinfulness

Before I went on the road full-time with Satellite Soul, I was the programming director at a church in Kansas City. One of my responsibilities was putting together artistic packages that could be paired up with every single sermon. Mostly a combination of songs, videos, and dramas, these packages were meant to ask a compelling question and rouse curiosity and interest in the sermon. For several years our creative team would survey the artistic landscape, trying to see how the culture treated issues of spirituality. It was fascinating. One Sunday we were going to be talking about heaven and hell. My job was to find clips from contemporary movies in which heaven and hell were discussed or portrayed in some fashion, then form them into a montage which would sketch the landscape of popular beliefs on that subject. I sat down one weekend with dozens of movies and started in. As I began compiling a mountain of clips, I began to marvel at the way a kind of "folk-theology" of heaven and hell had worked its way into our culture. Tons of movies had some sort of comment on heaven and hell, all of them very different from the true Christian story.

The movie *Tombstone* with Kurt Russell and Val Kilmer (who was, by the way, incredible in that movie) had a thread of a disembodied afterlife running through the entire film. In *What Dreams May Come* with Robin Williams and Cuba Gooding Jr., the hero leaves heaven and tracks down his wife, who is in hell, in order to bring her back to the good side. The film *Flatliners* had an all-star cast including Julia Roberts, Kevin Bacon, and Kiefer Sutherland. It's a story of a few curious med-school students who stop each other's hearts on purpose in order to explore the afterlife. Then they revive each other to tell their tales. Who could forget Kevin Costner in *Field of Dreams* and its portrayal of heaven just through the Iowa corn fields? Perhaps the most telling of all was the movie *Ghost* with Patrick Swayze, Demi Moore, and Whoopi Goldberg. The movie tells the story of a tortured man who has died, but remains trapped on earth as a ghost. He has to resolve several unfinished tasks before he can move on to heaven. The climactic ending comes when the antagonist dies and is dragged kicking and screaming through a portal to hell by animated demons. Then Swayze, who is a spirit with no body, knows it is time to leave when a light from heaven opens up a portal he can walk through. He says goodbye to his love, and honestly it is heart-wrenchingly sad and beautiful. There were lots of other films as well; those are just the ones I can remember.

As we watched this montage together as a church and talked about its meaning, it became clear the folk theology of heaven and hell we saw portrayed in film was not appreciably different from the ideas the congregation held. People's ideas were all over the board, but they seemed to be unaware of what the Bible actually has to say about the subject.

Here's my point: what we learned when we considered what the movies had to say about the afterlife versus what the Bible had to say about it was that most of the people in our church had been much more influenced by movies and the resulting folk theology than formal theology or the Scriptures, and our folk theology is really bad! The common American folk theology of heaven and hell is really just warmed-over Platonic dualism, yet it actually seemed to govern people's ideas about the subject more than the Bible did. Not only that, people had accepted some of those ideas without any critical thought and without referring to the Scripture to see what it taught. Most people felt no tension between their Christian beliefs and the beliefs we saw in those movies, even though there were obvious discrepancies.

FOLK THEOLOGY

Folk theology is quite possibly the most potent form of theology in contemporary evangelicalism. It is a term associated with a kind of unwritten theology which is widespread within a given community or culture. Folk theology is highly operative but generally unarticulated. It is received uncritically because it is simply part of how a community or culture shapes its people. Folk theology is typically received and internalized without any initiative shown on the part of the learner. Thus folk theology is deeply held by people who are generally unable to explain it, defend it, or critically assess it. In American evangelicalism, the most powerful and deeply held beliefs fall within the realm of folk theology. We find folk theology especially in music, film, and television. It weaves its way into the hearts and minds of the people in a given culture, and soon finds its way into the church. From there it governs the way people think and act, even the way they read and interpret the Scriptures. Folk theology exercises powerful control over the actions and attitudes of most people.

It doesn't have to be this way, of course. We could all simply begin to read the works of the great theologians. I wish everyone would be well versed in the writings of the great Reformation theologians like Luther, Calvin, and Wesley. I wish it would be commonplace to hear people discussing inaugurated eschatology on television. I'm a theology nerd—I totally admit that—so I wish Karl Barth was a consistent topic at dinner with friends instead of what crazy thing Lindsey Lohan did today or the other rubbish that seems to pervade our culture of fame. I wish people would read widely in theology, but unfortunately most of the people I know will not. We will rarely see those conversations on television or explore those topics at dinner with friends. So, for now at least, what we believe about God and spirituality is largely a result of our folk theology.

As an artist, I have always felt compelled to try and help shape the folk theology of our culture. Songwriting is all about shaping the imagination and tilling the soil so that people can see life in a different way. As a theologian, this desire to shape the folk theology of our culture found a concrete trajectory and theme. American folk theology must grow and develop in ways which are less individualistic and more open to the role of the community at large. Our folk theology needs to grow up. We need to engage it critically.

The folk theology of sin which lives in the subconscious of most evangelical Christians is chiefly concerned with individual sinful acts, sinful lifestyles, or sinful attitudes. When the typical evangelical Christian considers the problem of sin, we think of it in individualistic terms. We wonder about specific individual actions or attitudes and then ask if they are sinful. We think of it in the way I was taught in high school youth group: "Don't drink, or smoke, or chew, or go with girls who do," right? The folk theology of sin also treats sin like a blanket that covers the whole of humanity. Sin is often described as a condition common to all humanity. This actually comes much closer to a view of the Scriptures. Yet this is typically exploited in order to drive people to an awareness of their own sinfulness, and not the sinfulness of humanity as a whole.

Yet a mature doctrine of sin should recognize the social aspect of sin, and the way sin has become woven into the fabric of human societies. It would help us see the ways in which we are responsible for the actions of the groups and communities to which we belong. Typical individualistic folk theologies cannot bring people to the point where they are consciously aware of their complicity in social sins. If our theology, whether formal or folk, is going to be faithful to the story of God and the pursuit of God's kingdom it must address the need for a consciousness of social sin.

Luckily, we don't have to start from scratch, for this is the journey that Walter Rauschenbusch had to travel as well. Rauschenbusch firmly believed the doctrine of sin, as it was commonly held by American Protestants, needed to be challenged by the social gospel. He believed individualistic views of sin to be inadequate, a belief that I share today. Most contemporary evangelical Christians seem to have a good enough grasp on the personal aspect of sin, but we desperately need to understand the corporate nature of sin. Only then can we begin to live in step with the gospel Jesus came to preach. Don't get me wrong, we must not jettison our old views of personal sinfulness, we need them for sure. However, I do believe we must add to them the corporate aspect of sin if we are going to be faithful to the story of God. If we don't we will continue to allow the powers of sin and decay to have dominion over the earth. Most evangelical Christians already know what is involved in repentance from personal sin, yet few understand the importance of repenting from social sin. This is because many of us have no conscious awareness of it. This, I believe, is part of why evangelical Christians have not been more ardent in their pursuit of social justice. If we are to take the power of sin seriously, we have to be aware of its existence. This is fairly straightforward for an individual person living in a vacuum, but it gets complicated when we consider our common life.

THE AMERICAN FOLK THEOLOGY OF SIN

Much of the way we talk about sin and redemption in America today comes as a result of what is called the First Great Awakening, which happened in the 1730s. This period was marked by great Protestant revivals led by Jonathan Edwards and George Whitefield, who brought American Christianity a tactic called *revivalism*. In his book *Religion in the New*

World, George Wentz considers revivalism from an historical point of view and comes up with some very interesting conclusions. Wentz argues revival is not actually a movement of God so much as a reaction to societal change. When the conventions of social norms of society break down, great angst and confusion permeates the culture. Wentz says, "Revivals generally occur at a time when the accepted modes of order and meaning in society appear to be incapable of sustaining life."[1] The Christian story provides a unifying narrative in that environment. All of the Great Awakenings or revivals in America have come in these times of great cultural angst and confusion.

Later on, when the social upheaval subsides and social norms and customs cease their constant renegotiation, people stop responding. They did not come in droves as they had before because the culture was no longer in disequilibrium, so revivalist preachers began to *manufacture a crisis* for people to respond to. They began to preach more about personal sinfulness in a consistently convicting tone. They developed tactics like the "anxious bench" and the "altar call" in order to create a crisis moment for any willing individual. These practices began to shape the American folk theology of sin. It became completely individualistic. As a strategy for getting people to profess faith in Christ, revivalism was a very effective tactic. Here's the problem: revivalism generally involved no call to repentance for the social aspect of sin. It only dealt with personal sin. It was all rocket fuel and no oxygen. This dynamic of revivalism has had an indelible effect on contemporary American evangelicalism. It is largely concerned with forgiveness for the guilt of those sins and is individualistic through and through. As a result, the evangelical church began to lose its consciousness of social sin. Rauschenbusch was part of a generation of pastors who tried to correct this problem.

OPPOSITION RESEARCH

As Rauschenbusch and the other leaders of the new social gospel movement began to experience more influence, they were opposed and rejected by most evangelical leaders. Yet the rationale they used to oppose him back then has evaporated over the course of the past century. For instance, Isaac Haldeman, the pastor of First Baptist Church in New York City, was a highly influential evangelical. He published a pamphlet in 1911

1. Wentz, *Religion in the New World*, 174.

criticizing Rauschenbusch's work largely because of Rauschenbusch's use of the historical-critical method for biblical studies and interpretation. One hundred years ago, it was considered suspect for pastors to entertain some of the technical (back then they would say "scientific") inquiry to the Bible. But, today everybody does this. It's commonplace now. The practice Rauschenbusch was discredited for among evangelicals has gained nearly unanimous acceptance with those same people in the years since.[2] Isaac Haldeman's rationale for rejecting Rauschenbusch has evaporated.

Another example comes from the writings of George Fisher, the editor of what was a very popular evangelical periodical in its day called the *Gospel Message*. Fisher argued that Rauschenbusch had no business even calling his theology Christian and tried to have him fired from his seminary post. His attack was simply that Rauschenbusch did not speak about the gospel in the same way they did in the *Gospel Message*.[3] Today this line of thinking would be rejected by most evangelicals. Perhaps they would not choose to worship with a Roman Catholic, a Charismatic, or a Quaker, but most evangelicals would never claim those people are not even Christians. Evangelicalism itself has become very diverse. Fisher's critique would never hold water today because it would dismiss large swaths of the evangelical world.

These two critiques are emblematic of what I consider to be the mistaken, yet wholesale rejection of the social aspect of the gospel on behalf of American evangelical Christians. In a sense, what eventually occurred in the first few decades of the twentieth century was a split between two movements. On one side, the evangelical movement became chiefly concerned with personal sins. It was mostly rocket fuel without enough oxygen. The mainline movement became chiefly concerned with social sins. They were mostly oxygen without enough rocket fuel. Most evangelical Christians, myself included, have experienced a powerful inner transformation and a personal healing regarding our sinfulness. Yet, we remain blind to many of the larger injustices of society. The mainline church's lack of care to include the importance of a personal sin and redemption has cost them dearly as well. We have civil rights legislation in our country, but not enough personal transformation to abolish the racism in our hearts. One does not work without the other.

2. Evans, *Always but Coming*, 225.
3. Ibid., 227.

RAUSCHENBUSCH ON SIN

The desire to take sin seriously has always been an evangelical shibboleth. "If we could raise up some devout priest of the age of Amos or Isaiah to give his judgment on the theology of the prophets," Rauschenbusch once wrote, "he would probably assure us that these men doubtless meant well, but that they had no adequate sense of sin."[4] Yet the Jewish people vindicated the cause of the prophets and recognized that they spoke for God. Rauschenbusch's careful emphasis on the centrality of the doctrine of sin is no doubt meant to imitate the voice of the prophets while mitigating this criticism at the same time. "Any religious tendency or school of theology must be tested by the question," he wrote, "whether it does justice to the religious consciousness of sin." He conceded that some of his colleagues "put the blame for wrongdoing on the environment, and instead of stiffening and awakening the sense of responsibility in the individual, [taught] him to unload it on society."[5]

Rauschenbusch took the consciousness of sin very seriously, so much so that he turned the critique on the defenders of evangelical folk theology of sin, noting how their overemphasis on personal sinfulness has left them completely blind to the ways in which they are culpable for the social sins which plague society. He wrote,

> If the exponents of the old [read individualistic] theology have taught humanity an adequate consciousness of sin, how is it that they themselves have been blind and dumb on the master iniquities of human history? During all the ages while they were the theological keepers of the conscience of Christendom, the peasants in the country and the working class in the cities were being sucked dry by the parasitic classes of society, and war was damning poor humanity. Yet what traces are there in traditional theology that the minds of old-line theologians were awake to these magnificent manifestations of the wickedness of the human heart?[6]

Just as one cannot ignore personal sins, one cannot overlook the reality of social sin.

Rauschenbusch rightly believed it was not possible to live a life pleasing to God without, in his words, "a serious and humble sense of

4. Rauschenbusch, *Social Gospel*, 33.

5. Ibid., 32.

6. Ibid., 34.

sinfulness."[7] But this consciousness must include both the reality of personal sinfulness and social sinfulness. The consciousness of personal and social sin leads to the life of wisdom and allows us to see God. To lack it is a symptom of moral immaturity. To deny it is to deny reality.[8]

SIN IS A WEB

If we do not take seriously the social aspect of sin, we do not have a robust doctrine of sin. The guilt of sin is not only a stain on the person, but upon the people. Rauschenbusch wrote, "The weakness or the stubbornness of our will and the tempting situations of life combine to weave the tragic web of sin and failure of which we all make experience before we are through with our years."[9] Sin is a web. This was as keen an insight at the turn of the century as it is today. Sin is not merely the problem of the discrete individual person who willfully sins by what they have done and what they have left undone. Sin is a web of brokenness that permeates the cosmos. It has woven itself into the web of human relationships and social systems, perhaps even into our biological makeup. The reality of sin runs deep into the heart of the created order and it permeates the cosmos like a scarlet thread. It was the web of sin that so defined Rauschenbusch's view. If we do not carefully consider how sin is woven into our society, we cannot be fully conscious of sin. A lack of consciousness of social sin is a license to commit it.

Individualistic views of sin tend to ignore the way that sin has become bound up in the systems of our societies. Sin characterizes the whole of human relationships, and the fracture runs in all four directions. Individualistic views of sin cannot account for the myriad of ways in which sin pervades our political, economic, and legal systems. Every human system, at least on some level, bears the stain of human sin. It is woven into the foundation of every system's structure. It is not possible to account for this reality with an individualistic view of human sin. The consciousness of sin must extend beyond the realm of personal transgression, and draw out the web of sin in which we are all involved, and for which we have all cast our vote.

7. Ibid., 31.
8. Ibid., 24.
9. Ibid., 32.

An important piece of the puzzle is that we seem to be perhaps un-wittingly "voting" for this sinful system all the time.[10] We might say we abhor violence, yet we are entertained by images of it daily through televi-sion and movies. We might say we are for racial equality, but most of our churches remain segregated along racial lines.[11] We might say we care for the poor but few of us seem willing to lower our standard of living to offer the hope of economic redemption for the poorest of our neighbors—even in our own city. Statistics tell us that Christians do not live appreciably different lives than non-Christians in America.[12] Our minds might be in the right place on many issues, but we have yet to follow with our feet. We cannot greet the reality of sin with a cavalier, "the world is a broken place." We have broken it. We are still breaking it. We have voted for the chaos time and time again, and in so doing, we have given our proxy to fallen social systems and extended their tyranny to countless others. The consciousness of social sin has been scandalously overlooked by contem-porary evangelical folk theology.

As a result, social sins are not confronted by the church as they ought to be. The example that Rauschenbusch made famous was about a Mennonite farmer who was punished for having sold contaminated milk to his neighbors. Dirty milk was a real danger to the society, so red labels marked the cans of careless farmers whose milk was found to be contami-nated. If this happened too often, the farmer would not be able to stay in business and could lose his livelihood. One day a proper Mennonite farmer found his cans labeled red. In his embarrassment and anger the man swore an oath that his neighbors and fellow church members heard. Swearing an oath was considered sinful, a violation for which he was shunned by his faith community. But nothing was ever said about the fact that he had introduced cow-dung into the stomachs of innocent babies. The church was right there on the personal sin of swearing, yet totally dismissive of the social sin of endangering children. Even the commu-nity leaders—milk inspectors and health officers—recognized the man's serious social transgression, but the church did not.[13] Rauschenbusch's

10. Again, I'm indebted to Dr. Andy Johnson for the voting metaphor.

11. Sociologists Michael Emerson and Christian Smith have written convincingly about this reality in their book, *Divided by Faith*.

12. Ronald Sider makes this argument very effectively in his book, *The Scandal of the Evangelical Conscience*. Every evangelical Christian should read this book.

13. Rauschenbusch, *Social Gospel*, 35–36.

story shines a light on one of the serious shortcomings of the overly individualized Protestant doctrine of sin. We have ceded the recognition and responsibility for social sins to the state.

The church's lack of concern for most social sins should be a point of focus. After all, social sins are always the most destructive sins. Wars, corruption, systemic poverty, industrial pollution, and the like can cause widespread misery the likes of which individual sin can never match. For example, it is easy to blame the suffering of World War II on the sins of one maniacal German leader. But it is a more precarious assertion to note that the largely Protestant Christian German population failed to resist Hitler and thus should be held culpable as well. Dietrich Bonhoeffer and the confessing church were by far in the minority. Was it Hitler's personal sin or the German Christian's corporate sin that made the holocaust possible? The answer, I believe, must be "both."

Rauschenbusch was very careful not to become lax in regard to taking personal sins seriously. He admitted that some within the social gospel movement had swung the pendulum so far that there had been a loss of seriousness in regard to sin.[14] But he was committed not to allow this in his own heart and in those who would heed his influence. He rightly argued attention must be paid to "questions of public morality, on wrongs done by whole classes or professions of men [sic], on sins which enervate and submerge entire mill towns or agricultural states. These sins have been side-stepped by the old theology. We now have to make up for a fatal failure in past teaching."[15] *There is no turning to God without a turning toward each other; there is no turning toward each other without turning first to God.* Yet as long as the evangelical call for repentance is only couched in individualistic terms, we subvert the consciousness of social sin. We make justice a nonfactor in the story of God.

14. Ibid., 36.
15. Ibid.

7 A Mess of Our Own Making

I live in the western suburbs of Kansas City. The church I pastor does not own a building and currently meets in a high school, as we have for nearly a decade. The school is nearly brand new and it is an amazing facility. When it first opened, students were given PDAs on which they could take notes and access all of their textbooks electronically. Most of these kids go to college well prepared. I have a friend named Chris Jehle who lives fifteen miles from me, deeper into the city in one of the most violent zip codes in the country. He leads a ministry whose mission is to develop leaders who will someday help to turn their neighborhood back into a vibrant and healthy community. When those kids enter high school for the first time, they are met not with PDAs but with a pat-down, metal detectors, and an education that is simply not sufficient to prepare them for college. Jehle's volunteers and staff work with kids every day after school to plug the gaps in their education. In my neighborhood, we would never accept a school that did not adequately prepare our children for college. But it doesn't seem to bother us so much that it happens less than fifteen miles away in the same city. Our kids go off to college while the kids in Chris Jehle's neighborhood are left to fend for themselves, and we feel not the least bit responsible.

The question is, are we responsible for them? Is this our problem, way out here in the suburbs? The answer is yes, and the reason is tied to the concept of social sin. What the children in urban Kansas City are struggling against is social sin. Social sin is the kind of sin that has infected social systems. If an entire educational system systematically fails to nurture and educate its children year in and year out, it has become a broken and sinful system. I don't mean that to sound harsh or judgmental toward the teachers and administrators; they seem to be dedicated and many are devout Christians. But that is my point. The sin is not personal, it is social. The brokenness of humanity has worked its way into the educational system, and sinful systems perpetuate that brokenness. This is what happens when sin gets up a head of steam: it rolls through an entire social structure and imbeds itself in the systems and organization of the culture. The problem goes beyond personal sinfulness. Sin now lives in the broken educational system that cannot adequately educate its kids and help them find their way out of poverty. The innocent ones are just these little kids, especially when you consider the primary grades. They don't know about politics, they don't know about welfare, they don't understand the destructive nature of drugs and violence. They are doing exactly what we ask them to do; they are going to school, but the schools are broken.

We can name this problem many things, but as Christians we must learn to call it what it is: social sin. So, why are we responsible for it? Let me put it this way. It's interesting to me that it is easy to get white suburban evangelical Christians to go to the inner city to share the gospel. They are happy to do Bible school or evangelistic outreach events and share their faith. But it is very difficult to get them to go to the inner city to address the failing educational system. We in the suburbs are happy to address personal sin with the good news of a personal relationship with Christ. But we are unequipped and unmotivated to address social sins with the good news. We are surely meant to bring the good news of God's redemption to those who are drowning in personal sin, i.e., outreach events, vacation Bible school, etc. Yet we seem unaware that we are also responsible to bring the good news to those who are drowning in social sin, i.e., get involved in their educational system; lobby the government; volunteer in the schools; move to the neighborhood as missionaries to be good neighbors; plug the gaps in the social safety net where children are falling through all the way to the ground, etc.

But, this is not what we do. We ignore social sin because we can. We ignore it because the only gospel we know is individualistic, and this does not address social sin. We do not know the gospel that confronts broken social systems—or systemic evil—with the good news of God's redemption. The power of evil has become bound up in the systems of our society. The individualistic gospel actually supports the callous attitude toward those who are stuck in systemic poverty. It blames individuals for their own plight. But it does not recognize that sin is always moving throughout the system. They are struggling with a sin which is not only personal, but social as well; it is bound up in our social systems.

The gospel must address not only the personal manifestation of sin, but the social manifestation of sin as well.

Evangelical Christians are fond of saying the reason things are so bad in blighted and poverty stricken urban areas is because of sin. They are right about that. But they are wrong in their assumption that it is only the personal sins of the drug users, gang members, and drug dealers that are responsible. We are responsible as well. It is a mess of our own making, for we have created and supported the corrupt systems that make poverty inevitable. And, inexplicably, we let ourselves off the hook. Our kids are fine. They're going to go to college. Don't think for a minute that those of us living in the suburbs would put up with schools that systematically fail to prepare our kids for college. We would do something about it. You've heard the axiom, "Give a man a fish and he'll eat for a day. Teach a man to fish and he'll eat for a lifetime." Often the man who has learned to fish comes to the water's edge only to be greeted with great big sign which says, "No Fishing." Those signs are not just *his* problem, they are *our* problem. Many of us are responsible for those signs in the first place. They are the evidence of our callousness toward the way sin lives as a present force within our human social systems. Those kids in urban Kansas City, they are our problem. They need the gospel to redeem them personally and socially.

SOLIDARITY WITH FUTURE GENERATIONS

Understanding sin and evil as a present force will help us to recognize our corporate culpability for the way we organize our common life. Rauschenbusch believed us to be responsible for the institutions we create and pass on to successive generations. He believed one of the greatest needs for the church of his time was to recognize its responsibility for this world. The human vocation is to fill it, till it, and keep it. We are responsible for how things turn out for the next generation. As Christians, we must take this seriously. Rauschenbusch wrote, "One of the greatest tasks in religious education reserved for the social gospel is to spread in society a sense of the solidarity of successive generations and a sense of responsibility for those who are to come after us."[1] We are not simply responsible to pass our faith on to our own children. We are also responsible to build systems of economics, politics, education, etc., that are just.

1. Rauschenbusch, *Social Gospel*, 43.

Micah asks the right question, "What does the Lord require of you?" Our answer must be like his: "To act justly, and to love mercy, and to walk humbly with your God."[2] To act justly is not merely an individual choice wherein each of us treats the other as we want to be treated, nor is it about punishing the guilty criminal. Justice concerns the systems which we have created and operate within. Are they just? When they are not, they are sinful systems.

I once heard a story about a few friends who were standing on the banks of a beautiful but icy-cold river admiring the view, when they noticed a man floating down the river near the bank, screaming for help. They formed a human chain to catch him as he came by and rescued him from the freezing water. As they were all still recovering, they noticed another person, a woman this time, in the same predicament so they saved her as well. Immediately, they saw a couple of children floating toward them, then another man, another woman, and this went on for awhile until the people were all soaked and exhausted. Finally, somebody suggested that instead of just pulling people out of the freezing river, maybe they should send somebody to find out who was throwing people in. The point of the story is this: the gospel of personal salvation (think Billy Graham and rocket fuel), is like pulling people out of the water. The social gospel (think Martin Luther King Jr. and oxygen), is like stopping people from getting thrown in. The true gospel is not an either/or proposition, it is both/and.

A doctrine of social sin will also help demonstrate that sin's most powerful manifestations will typically be its social manifestations, i.e. sin that has become imbedded in the systems of culture, government, economics, etc. A doctrine of sin which is individualistic can only address personal sin. A doctrine of social sin can properly emphasize both the personal and the social aspects of human sinfulness.[3] A doctrine of social sin will also make it necessary to find solidarity with past and future generations as well as the present one, allowing us to focus "on the present and active sources of evil."[4] It was Rauschenbusch's conviction this would make it possible to preach both a personal and social gospel simultaneously.

2. Micah 6:8.

3. Rauschenbusch, *Social Gospel*, 50–54.

4. Ibid., 44.

Sin is always a conflict between selfish desire and the common good. Rauschenbusch wrote, "The sinful mind, then, is the unsocial and anti-social mind."[5] Therefore the climax of sin is not the person who sneers at religion and denies the reality of God, but the social groups which dominate, oppress, or marginalize great swaths of people to satisfy their own agenda.

SPIRITUAL AUTHORITY OF SOCIETY OVER THE PERSON

Part of why Rauschenbusch consistently emphasized social alongside personal sin was what he called the "spiritual authority of society over its members."[6] Social groups have incredible power. We have trained our youth ministers to point out the power of peer pressure to our teenagers, but we have not learned how to make ourselves aware of the ways in which we are all manipulated and influenced by social forces. Social conventions can *suppress the natural checks* for sin and *hide the consequences of sin* as well. Sin can be ignored if society deems so, which constitutes an important and problematic social sin itself. If a society does not have some punishment for a sin, then it must not be a sin, right? This ability to ignore evil and injustice constitutes a powerful spiritual authority that a society can exercise over its members.

For example, consider the evangelical church's absolute rejection of Jesus's teaching concerning nonviolence. In the Sermon on the Mount Jesus advocates for a nonviolent response to evil; not that evil wouldn't be resisted, but that Christians must not resist violently. Early Christians seemed to take this teaching very seriously. There is no historical evidence that Christians served in the military before AD 170–180, and after that it was exceedingly rare. Origen, an early church father, had to defend Christians against Celsus, an early opponent of Christianity who was attacking them for their lack of military service. Origen argued, "You cannot demand military service of Christians any more than you can of priests. We do not go forth as soldiers," (Against Celsus VIII.7.3). Justin Martyr wrote, "we who formerly used to murder one another do not only now refrain from making war upon our enemies, but also, that we may not lie nor deceive our examiners, willingly die confessing Christ," (First Apology of Justin Martyr, ch. 39). All throughout the writings of the first

5. Ibid., 50.
6. Ibid., 61.

few centuries of the church, one can find a consistent message against violence of any kind. We find these in the teachings of Justyn Martyr, Irenaeus, Clement of Alexandria, Tertullian, Origen, Hippolytus, and many others. Early Christians were prohibited from violence. Nonviolent resistance of evil was the typical teaching in the first century, and Christians were criticized for it. After Constantine, and more pervasively during the rise of the modern nation-state, Christian theology had to adjust its convictions in order to allow Christians to fight in wars. After centuries of this teaching, those who hold to the conviction of nonviolent resistance of evil have now been relegated to the station of the radical, even though their position is clearly advocated by Christ in the Sermon on the Mount, and by the first few centuries of his followers. War is now considered noble in our society. Rauschenbusch noted war had become "the supreme test of manhood and of the worth of a nation."[7] Nonviolence is considered cowardly or naïve. The theological convictions of the church have become so privatized and individualized that there is no widespread contemporary evangelical critique of the violence that is continually exercised in the name of the state. Our society has trumped the clear teachings of Jesus on nonviolence through its spiritual authority. Forget the Beatles, the nation-state is bigger than Jesus.

This is an example of sin that is transmitted socially, and which has been significantly fueled by individualistic and privatized notions of Christianity. Those who oppose violence on principle are held in check and branded as radicals. Their voices are pressed to the margins of society. The resulting idealized view of *war* is actually just an idealized view of *sin,* which is now generally espoused by the church itself. The idealization of sin becomes the way social systems, even the church itself, can transmit and perpetuate sin through control of the persons who belong to the group.

Rauschenbusch recognized the power of society over human behavior. Social groups can cause "good people to do bad things" or "bad people to do good things," and they exhibit themselves as the most powerful ethical forces known to humankind. They have spiritual authority over the lives of the individual persons within them. Social groups can use their power to raise people up, as is the case with groups like the Salvation Army or the United Way. They can also use their power to drag people

7. Ibid., 65.

down. They can even cause people to act in ways they would not typically act, such as in a crowd at a professional football game screaming "tear his head off," or traffic-jam on the freeway cursing the "idiots" in our way. Those are fairly benign examples, but what about the other social groups to which we belong: political parties, the military, fraternities and sororities, alumni organizations, professional organizations, etc.? To what end are they trained? Are they redemptive? Are they part of the solution or part of the problem? Most importantly, what sort of power do they have over us? Do we give them sovereignty reserved for God and the community of believers? Is their agenda the common good or are they really meant to build up the resumes and portfolios of their members?

SUPER-PERSONAL FORCES AND SOCIETY AT LARGE

Rauschenbusch consistently appealed to the Old Testament prophets as evidence that things were not always this way. He noted the prophets "saw their nation as a gigantic personality which sinned, suffered, and repented," as a group.[8] This image of a whole community of people who sin, suffer, repent, and act within history not simply as individuals, but as a group is an example of what Rauschenbusch called a "super-personal force." Individualistic theology, Rauschenbusch noted, cannot "recognize and observe spiritual entities beyond the individual,"[9] thus it cannot discern the presence and power which super-personal forces exercise over society at large. The super-personal force exists with one purpose in mind: to actively use its collective influence to change culture in ways that serve its agenda. This is the very principle, for instance, which lies behind the political action committee. They gain wide membership and use the proxy of their members to shape society as a whole. Rauschenbusch notes that this is precisely how super-personal forces become, "the most powerful ethical forces in our communities."[10]

Not only are super-personal forces more powerful than individual entities, super-personal entities are more widespread than the person. Their lifespan far outstretches that of an individual person's life. They do not cease to exist if a few members die or leave the group; and they are

8. Ibid., 69.
9. Ibid.
10. Ibid., 72.

relatively impervious to critique and stricture from outside the group. Humans continually interact with various super-personal forces and are often swept up in their inertia without ever realizing the consequences of the actions of the group.

When super-personal forces are trained toward the common good, and thus the kingdom of God, they are super-personal forces for good. When they are trained toward any form of selfishness, they can easily become what Rauschenbusch termed "super-personal forces of evil."[11] Generally, super-personal forces of evil have fallen from a more lofty purpose or existence. An organization founded to aid the health and well-being of its members may fall to corruption and ensnare otherwise good people in its trap. People who organize to overthrow tyrannical or despotic governments often find themselves resorting to the same tactics as the previous rulers in order to keep in power. Rauschenbusch continually points to the love of monetary or social gain, love of fame, or love of power as chief among reasons social organizations that started out with a redemptive purpose later become corrupt super-personal forces of evil.

Once a super-personal force has become corrupted by sin, it is forced into the position of having to resist its members' efforts to gain freedom and justice. Thus it stands in opposition to the kingdom of God. These forces hold god-like sovereignty over the lives of their members. Jesus's mission of redemption included these super-personal forces. In his coming out speech in Luke 4, Jesus read from the scroll of Isaiah and announced his mission: "The Spirit of the Lord is upon me, because he has anointed me to preach good news to the poor. He has sent me to proclaim freedom for the prisoners and recovery of sight for the blind, to release the oppressed, to proclaim the year of the Lord's favor."[12] Christ *named* the super-personal forces of evil in Luke 4: poverty, oppression, spiritual blindness, and captivity. *When he named them he marked them for redemption*, and declared his sovereignty over them. It must be recognized that the super-personal forces of evil were in Christ's mind from the very beginning of his ministry.

Super-personal forces of evil have powerful wide-sweeping effects on not only the person, but on the entire economy of human life. This problem is much more basic to the Christian faith than most of us will ever realize. It cuts to the very heart of the gospel, the death and resur-

11. Ibid., 69.
12. Luke 4:16–19; (NIV).

rection of Jesus. We've already seen that Jesus named the social forces in Luke 4 and in so doing, he marked them for redemption. Rauschenbusch notes that one can clearly see the ways in which Christ himself suffered under the effects of social sin. Rauschenbusch wrote this incredible list of the social sins that combined to send Jesus to the cross. When we say that Christ *bore our sins*, we do not mean individual sins only, but social sins as well. These are the social sins Rauschenbusch believed Christ bore for humanity:

1. *Religious Bigotry*: the lust for power and control demonstrated by the religious leaders that finds its expression through persecution of those with lesser or no power in the organization.

2. *Graft and Political Power*: those who exploit religious and political power for monetary gain.

3. *Corruption of Justice*: inequality between rich and poor, concentration of wealth, power, and capital in the hands of the few on the backs of the many.

4. *Mob Spirit and Mob Action*: when the restraints of self-criticism and self-control are ceded to the emotions of the masses, we have what Rauschenbusch calls "the social spirit gone bad."[13]

5. *Militarism*: those who live by the sword, often lending warped religious rationale for violence.

6. *Class Contempt*: a tendency to blame lower classes and powerless people for their own predicament which blinds people to their guilt in the matter.[14]

The fact that these evils were present in Palestine during Christ's day, and are present in our day as well, speaks to the universality of social sin. These were the social sins that Rauschenbusch believed combined to crush and kill Jesus. "Insofar as the personal sins of men have contributed to the existence of these public sins, he [Christ] came into collision with the totality of evil in mankind [*sic*]."[15] By continuing to participate in the sins of the past and perpetuating the very same sinful social systems that

13. Rauschenbusch, *Social Gospel.*, 254.

14. Ibid., 248–58.

15. Ibid., 248.

led to Christ's death, *we make ourselves personally and socially culpable for the death of Christ*. Rauschenbusch said, "Insofar then as we, by our conscious actions or passive consent, have repeated the sins which killed Jesus, we have made ourselves guilty of his death. If those who actually killed him stood before us, we could not wholly condemn them, but would have to range ourselves with them."[16] Society had such a powerful spiritual force, even his closest disciples didn't dare to stand with Christ in the end. Isn't it naïve to think we are somehow untainted by those same forces?

THE KINGDOM OF EVIL

The ultimate sinful super-personal force is what Rauschenbusch calls the "Kingdom of Evil."[17] The Kingdom of Evil is the complex of super-personal forces of evil that have converged to perpetuate the power of sin. The essence of the Kingdom of Evil is the *common human solidarity of sinfulness* that pervades the entire cultural milieu. In our day, as well as in Rauschenbusch's day, this can be seen as an indictment of nearly every way we have ordered our common life together in our society. All of the systems—economic, political, educational, legal, medical, social, etc.—are implicated and involved in the Kingdom of Evil. The church has not resisted them because the church has not recognized them for what they are. The unquestioned sovereignty which the super-personal forces of evil come to exercise in the lives of the people of any culture, especially a culture in which religious life is meant to remain personalized and privatized, renders each person passive and unable to resist the Kingdom of Evil. So how can it be counteracted?

In order to address the Kingdom of Evil, we must certainly take responsibility for our personal sins. But taking responsibility for our personal sins alone will not have a serious effect on the Kingdom of Evil. We must also take responsibility for our social sins. There must be a corporate repentance for the fact that we all participate, as Rauschenbusch says, "to the working principles of the Kingdom of Evil, and do not counteract it with all our strength."[18] To a certain extent I'm sure we don't counteract it because of greed, sloth, materialism, etc. But I think the major reason we

16. Ibid., 259.

17. Ibid., 77.

18. Ibid., 92.

do not counteract the Kingdom of Evil is that we do not recognize it as it hides beneath the guise of the institutions and systems of our society, nor do we challenge ourselves to recognize it in what feels and seems to us like normal society. Rauschenbusch gave himself passionately to the cause of unmasking and opposing the super-personal forces of evil. It was these forces, wolves in sheep's clothing he believed, who opposed him and I believe continue to oppose any social awareness in evangelical Christianity.

Most importantly we must remember that Jesus opposed the Kingdom of Evil. He exposed and resisted systemic sin. He did so not with the sword, but by allowing evil to do its worst to Him. Evil exhausted itself on Christ, and he bore our sin—social and personal—on the cross. The call to evangelism is a call to bear witness to the redemption of Jesus Christ. We do this personally *and* socially, or we fail to live up to the example set by Jesus.

8 Corporate Salvation

If evangelicals stop advocating for personal salvation, the cause becomes lost. Yet it is important to notice the salvation Jesus came to enact and proclaim did involve a turning from a life of self-gratification to a life focused on love of God and neighbor—God and neighbor. Personal sin must be considered in regard to both God and neighbor. We might sin against God. We might also sin against our neighbor. Both are in view when we talk about the impact of personal salvation. As we move on to consider the ways in which God may have provided for the salvation of social bodies—or corporate salvation—we must never leave personal salvation behind. It is essential. Any doctrine of corporate salvation that leaves personal salvation behind is incomplete.

Conversely, any doctrine of salvation that focuses solely on the personal aspect to the exclusion of the corporate aspect is incomplete. So far we've explored ways in which sin exists on the personal level as well as the super-personal level. Sin is not always simply a personal transgression against God or other people. Sin has become bound up in the systems of our world. The Christian story insists that God has addressed both our personal and corporate sins through the birth, life, teaching, death, and resurrection of Jesus Christ. God is not only concerned about the personal manifestations of sin but the corporate as well. Therefore the gospel involves this good news that God has made provision for those corporate manifestations of sin through Jesus. Just as our doctrines of sin must consider both the personal and corporate aspects, our doctrines of salvation must do the same.

BAPTISM AND SWITCHING STORIES

In 1994, President Habyarimana of Rwanda was killed when his plane was shot down on final approach into Kigali Airport. Within moments of his death, the presidential guard began killing all political opposition to their planned takeover of the government. The next day, members of the Hutu tribal militia began the systematic killing of all fellow Rwandans who were a part of their rival Tutsi tribe. Over the course of the next one hundred days, the violence spread throughout the entire country and some eight hundred thousand Rwandans—mostly Tutsis and moderate Hutus—had been murdered in cold blood—genocide. Most Americans scarcely even knew the story until learning about it in the highly acclaimed movie *Hotel Rwanda* in 2004. This movie brought the heartbreaking reality to all of us, and with it the realization that our government knew about the genocide, yet did nothing to stop it.

In his book *Mere Discipleship*, Lee Camp reminds us that before the genocide of 1994, Rwanda was best known in the Christian world as a case study for the success of world missions. In the 1930s there had been a massive conversion to Christianity among both the government leadership as well as the people. The conversion to Christianity was so complete that at the time of the genocide nearly 90 percent of the population professed to be Christians. Yet the gospel exported to Rwanda by Western Christians was largely individualistic, trained on the winning of heaven and immortality. Nothing had been taught to them concerning their identity as the people of God and the bonds of brotherly and sisterly love integral to the way of Christ. Even after conversion, the people's primary allegiance was still tied to their tribe over and against all other allegiances, including their Christian identity. How could it be that a nation of Christians could commit such atrocities? Why was the gospel so weak and fruitless that it could not quell such unthinkable ethnic violence?[1]

Through Christ we have become sons and daughters of God, and therefore brothers and sisters. Just like in *The Godfather*, we never take sides against the family. No bond can be stronger than this one, no allegiance more important than our allegiance to God and each other. Paul's metaphor of adoption into the Christian family was all but lost on the Christians of Rwanda. I wonder, is it lost on us as well? We might be tempted to dismiss this as a rare case of uneducated radical tribes in a primitive country. Yet the American story includes a very similar scene. In the Civil War, allegiance to the Confederacy or the Union seemed quite enough for Christian brothers to take up arms against one another. Perhaps it was not ethnic violence, but Christians killed Christians out of

1. Camp, *Mere Discipleship*, 19–20.

an allegiance to the North or South that usurped all allegiances to God and each other.

Rauschenbusch noted, "In primitive Christianity baptism stood for a conscious break with pagan society."[2] Baptism was a public renunciation of citizenship in the Roman Empire and a joining with the people of God. The image is death and resurrection. Through our baptism we are dead to our old allegiances—which, by the way, always serve to divide us and pit us against one another—and alive to a new family through our adoption by Christ. This new family rejects the broken down rules that human communities have come to live by. They now embody a whole new way of being a human being. Rauschenbusch rightly said, "Baptism was the dramatic expression of an inward consent and allegiance to the higher standards of life which were to prevail in the Messianic community. It was the symbol of a revolutionary movement."[3] Baptism had become the symbol of a revolutionary movement to which one gave total unreserved allegiance. No identity could usurp it.

The Hutus told a story about the way the world was. In that story the Tutsis were to blame for all of their problems. The South told a story about the way the world was. In that story the North was to blame for all of their problems. We all tell a story about the way the world is. Who is to blame for all our problems in the story we tell? Do we blame society? Do we blame the devil? Do we blame the liberals? Do we blame the conservatives? Do we blame the Muslims? Most of us blame everybody but ourselves and then turn those we blame into our enemy. This is not the way of Christ. When we joined with Christ in our baptism, we switched stories. We died to our old social identities and allegiances. We stopped living in the dominant story of our culture that tells us all kinds of crazy stuff about who we are, what the world is like, and how to live our lives. We renounce all rival stories and give ourselves unreservedly to become a part of the story of God. In God's story we stop blaming and start to live a life of radical acceptance and love. We engender not only a new belief system but a new social ethic defined by the teaching of Christ.

The act of baptism is a radical identification with Jesus as Lord and with the people of God. From that point forward when the person comes out of the water and says, "These are my people," what he or she must

---

2. Rauschenbusch, *Social Gospel*, 99.

3. Ibid., 198.

be referring to is first and foremost the people of God and the church, not the state or any other social entity. Salvation is not simply an imputation of personal righteousness before God, but a comprehensive new social identity. John Howard Yoder argued as much in *The Politics of Jesus* where he wrote, "My purpose is not to reverse a prior error by claiming that justification is *only* social. I am objecting to a particular polemical application of the traditional doctrine, which used it to *exclude* the ethical and social dimensions."[4] Yoder did not wish to deny the personal dimension of salvation. He merely called into question the idea that personal salvation can be adequately considered apart from its social aspect, as traditional Reformed and evangelical theologies have assumed. Rauschenbusch espoused an identical view of salvation saying, "If our exposition of the super-personal agents of sin and of the kingdom of evil is true, then evidently a salvation confined to the soul and its personal interests is an imperfect and only partly effective salvation."[5] This perfectly describes why the salvation which the Rwandan people experienced was not powerful enough to reject the notion of genocide. It was only partly effective salvation. It was all rocket fuel and no oxygen.

Recognizing the social aspect of salvation would effectively modify the way in which we discern the salvation of discrete persons. Rauschenbusch always maintained that one of the most damaging problems in American society was the Christian who was saved and reconsecrated several times, and yet was still essentially worthless to the kingdom of God. To profess true salvation, thus to bring our baptism to its intended goal, we must judge the authenticity of our conversion according to its social manifestations, not simply its inner, personal ones. True Christian salvation involves a simultaneous turning toward God and humanity. It is accomplished in and through Christ and is not the work of the human heart. It is graciously empowered and received as pure gift. But if we only accept the gift personally and ignore its corporate aspect, we have not enjoyed full salvation.

MISUNDERSTANDING RAUSCHENBUSCH

Many evangelicals who become aware of Walter Rauschenbusch and the social gospel movement accuse him of saying one does not need personal

4. Yoder, *The Politics of Jesus*, 215.
5. Rauschenbusch, *Social Gospel*, 95.

salvation, only social salvation. While speaking at the Pew Forum on Religion and Public Life in Key West, Florida in May of 2005, Rick Warren, author of the best-selling book *The Purpose Driven Life*, made the typical critique. Warren said, "There is a fellow named Walter Rauschenbusch, who is the man who came up with the term 'social gospel.' Rauschenbusch was a liberal theologian and he basically said we don't need this stuff about Jesus anymore; we don't need the cross; we don't need salvation; we don't need atonement; we just need to redeem the social structures of society and if we do that people will automatically get better. This is basically Marxism in a Christian form."[6]

Warren's critique of Rauschenbusch is what many of us were taught to believe. The problem is that it just isn't true. What Rauschenbusch actually said was, "the salvation of the individual is, of course, an essential part of salvation."[7] He included a whole chapter on personal salvation in *A Theology for the Social Gospel*, stating clearly "our discussion cannot pass personal salvation by. We might possibly begin where the old gospel leaves off, and ask our readers to take all the familiar experiences and truths of personal evangelism and religious nurture for granted in what follows."[8] What Rauschenbusch actually argued for with respect to personal salvation was that, "The social gospel furnishes new tests for religious experience."[9] If a person professes to a conversion experience, yet they do not seem to have changed in their approach to their fellow human beings, then we might want to consider the authenticity of their experience. Whatever personal religious experience one might claim to have had, it had to undergo the fruit test. What kind of fruit does it bear? If it does not bear the fruit of love toward neighbor, it was not authentically Christian.

This is exactly the meaning of Jesus's teaching in Matthew 25. Those who are sent away in the parable of the sheep and the goats are the ones who did not turn toward the hungry, the stranger, the naked, the sick, and the prisoner. Christ warns us that our choices have eternal consequences. The overly individualized view of salvation widely espoused in evangelicalism seems to ignore the clear teaching of Jesus. This was

6. Warren, "Myths of the Megachurch."

7. Rauschenbusch, *Social Gospel*, 95.

8. Ibid., 96.

9. Ibid.

Rauschenbusch's critique of revivalism. He said, "We have the highest authority for the fact that men [*sic*] may grow worse by getting religion."[10] He critiqued movements which were rooted in crisis evangelism because he thought they were "calculated to produce skin deep changes."[11]

Our recognition of the social aspect of sin necessitates the recognition of the social aspect of God's plan for salvation. Salvation according to Jesus, involved two simultaneous movements in love: toward God and toward neighbor. Again, Matthew 25:46 says judgment is reserved for those who refuse their neighbor in need. Matthew 12:28-31 irreducibly joins loving God and loving others and calls them the key to drawing near to the kingdom of God. One cannot love God if one does not love their neighbor. One cannot love their neighbor if they do not love God. And, most importantly, one cannot love at all unless they are first seized by the love of God. "Salvation," Rauschenbusch argued, "must be a change which turns a man [*sic*] from the self to God and humanity."[12] When we submit to God, we submit to the common good.[13]

I would argue that Rauschenbusch was intentionally vague on what he believed the essence of personal salvation to be because he did not want to get into an argument about a Baptist versus Lutheran, or Catholic versus Anglican view of how personal salvation should work. In essence he was saying: Make whatever moves you want to make concerning Christology, Soteriology, and the personal view of salvation. Follow your tradition on this aspect, but you must add to it the social dimension for it to be complete. His assertion was that none of the modes of personal salvation were complete if they failed to recognize the social aspect. His agenda was not to argue about the mechanics of personal salvation, but to argue for the addition of the social aspect of salvation to whatever form of personal salvation one was committed to. I believe this is another reason we cannot call Rauschenbusch a typical liberal. He was a Baptist who held to a typical Baptist view of personal salvation throughout his whole life. He merely recognized that one aspect of personal salvation required a move toward our neighbor in love.

This movement toward the other in love cannot be simply a heart commitment. It has to work itself out in the way we live our lives.

10. Ibid., 96.

11. Ibid., 97.

12. Ibid.

13. Ibid., 99.

Rauschenbusch was decried in his day for being a socialist. It's interesting to read the rhetoric now, a full century later, because it seems so myopic. Rauschenbusch once laid out seven measures he would like to see enacted. These would serve not to convert capitalism into socialism, but to curb capitalism by helping it serve the common good. His seven suggestions were:

1. Property tax on land owned.

2. Municipal ownership of natural monopolies such as water, gas, electric, and roads.

3. Public telegraph and post office to allow people to control their own communications.

4. Public funding of education, libraries, museums, parks, playgrounds.

5. Breaking up the over-accumulation of wealth in the hands of a few via inheritance tax.

6. Organization of labor unions for the advancement and management of industry.

7. Safe labor regulations such as: regulating the length of the work week, requiring safe and sanitary working conditions, prevention of child labor, etc.[14]

If these sound familiar it is because they are generally accepted as part of contemporary American society. Ironically, nearly everything Rauschenbusch lobbied for so long ago has now become a normal part of our political and economic life. Parcel post, publicly funded parks and recreation, public transportation, municipal housing programs, social security, occupational safety standards, progressive inheritance taxes, child labor laws, the right to organize labor—these are generally accepted as the fruits of living in a free society. The agenda Walter Rauschenbusch fought for a century ago has become a valuable part of our society. This is an example of what can happen if corporate sin is addressed and God is allowed to redeem the systems of a society.

14. Sharpe, *Walter Rauschenbusch*, 212–13.

THE FAILURE OF INDIVIDUALISTIC SALVATION

Evangelical folk theology is not completely blind to the reality of systemic evil. Yet the solution typically offered is that the individual members of the social body must each experience a personal conversion. Once each individual member of the social body becomes saved, then the social body will become saved as well. This is the typical atomistic approach of the Enlightenment, but it is the Achilles heel for individualistic notions of personal salvation. It just doesn't play out that way in real life.

Consider this practical example: A large industrial company pollutes the environment and puts the health of the community at risk. The common laborer in the company might blame management—they gave the orders. The head of the company might plausibly blame his board of directors—they pressured him to act. The board of directors might blame the chairman of the board—he only had his eye on the balance sheet. The chairman of the board points to the stockholders—they demand higher stock prices. But the average stockholder is likely invested in mutual funds, so they don't even know which specific stocks they own, much less that they've invested in a company that pollutes the environment. The personal salvation of the shareholder will have no effect on a company that has been ravaging the environment. Every person from top to bottom could become converted to the gospel of individual salvation, and yet the super-personal force of evil would roll on undaunted and unopposed. All of the participants along the structure of the super-personal force of evil can claim innocence and blame the social system (often conceived of as the "fallen world"), thereby evading any complicity or blame. This is how the Kingdom of Evil is built. This is its most frightening and damaging characteristic, and it is unopposed by doctrines of sin and salvation, which are trained on the individual without regard for the social aspect of sin. Somebody must work to change the culture of greed which perpetuates a system which will ultimately harm the world we've been charged to keep.

If we need more proof that social bodies can have many, if not a majority of members who have experienced personal salvation and yet willingly participate in an evil an enterprise, we need only to look at the history of the United States of America. As a super-personal force, America was established, in large part, by Protestant Christians who came to the new world seeking, among other things, religious freedom. As the colonies grew and developed into a sovereign nation, the churches continued their work in North America by converting people to Christianity. Revivalism and the Great Awakenings helped to establish a country virtually filled with people who had experienced some sort of personal salvation. Yet this same super-personal force systematically eliminated an entire Native American culture, even its women and children, using horrific means to do so. These people who were regenerate in the eyes of individualistic theology prospered on the backs of African slaves for centuries, exploiting their "free" labor for massive economic gain. Privatized religious convictions and conversions failed to adequately resist the actions of the group.[15] America was at once filled with Christians and enslaving or killing masses of people.

Without the gospel of social salvation alongside it, the gospel of personal salvation is powerless to resist super-personal forces of evil. As a result, the gospel of individual conversion that pervades the American evangelical church has become an unwitting participant in the Kingdom of Evil.[16] An entirely individualistic conception of sin ultimately leads to a religious system that is self-concerned and as such, is ill equipped to address social sin. In that eventuality, it becomes essential to recognize the teaching of the Prophets and of Jesus, both of whom treated sin as a "present force" and called for both corporate and personal repentance. Thus conceived, it seems prudent to urge the church to acknowledge our common solidarity of sin as well as our complicity with and failure to adequately resist the Kingdom of Evil. Only this solidarity and recognition of social and individual sin can lead to a robust doctrine of salvation.

Salvation involves an attitude of love toward fellow human beings, recognizing their value to God, living in a conscious loving coordination with other people. The turning from selfishness is never simply a turning to God, but always a turning to God and to others whom God greatly values. This necessitates a rejection of the sinful institutions with which the person has been previously identified. Rauschenbusch steadfastly maintained that authentic religious experiences were not meant simply

15. Although it must be said that Christians worked to quell the practice of slavery, we must remember those Christians who resisted slavery possessed a social concept of sin. The church never addressed the genocide of Native Americans until long after it was over, and again it was addressed by Christians who held a social view of sin.

16. For a full iteration of this concept look to William T. Cavanaugh, *Torture and Eucharist*.

to edify the life of the believer, but to draw them out toward the "other." He said, "solidaristic religious experience is more distinctively Christian than individualistic religious experience."[17] Rauschenbusch rightly recognized the fear of personal damnation or punishment is in essence an ultimately selfish motivation for salvation. He called it "self interest on a higher level."[18] But true regeneration, including both the personal and social conversion of the person, must have an eye toward all of humanity and her social institutions to be authentic.

There are many biblical metaphors from which to draw upon to get a picture for what it means to experience salvation in the complete sense. The dominant metaphor in evangelicalism is the one introduced by Paul. It is a forensic term called *justification*. Justification is a legal metaphor meant to express a change in personal legal status before God. This is an important metaphor. But there are others. The term *adoption* is used. Adoption comes from the realm of family life. It is an important social metaphor for salvation. The term *conversion* is used to convey an active break with an old way of being human and a turning to a whole new way of life. It too is a term with social implications. *Regeneration* is perhaps the strongest term associated with personal salvation. Rauschenbusch wrote, "We call the change 'regeneration' when we think of it as an act of God within us, creating a new life."[19] No single term can dominate the others. Yet in contemporary evangelicalism, justification controls, even mutes all other metaphors. We must come to recognize that all of these terms (and more) are necessary to convey the great mystery that is our salvation through Christ. Moreover, we must come to see how each one can shed light on different social aspects of salvation that can be lost if our only metaphor is justification.

17. Rauschenbusch, *Social Gospel*, 108.
18. Ibid.
19. Ibid., 99.

9   The Good News of the Kingdom of God

Let's say you are with me so far. You agree that the true power of the gospel is at the nexus of the personal and corporate. It takes rocket fuel and oxygen to make this ship move. Where is it going? What is the size and scope of God's redemptive project? The answer is the Kingdom of God.

One of my favorite writers is a man named Aaron Sorkin. He created and wrote most of the popular television show *The West Wing*. Sorkin also wrote the 2010 motion picture called *The Social Network*, about the creators of Facebook. While promoting the movie, Sorkin did an interview on a late night television show in which he said, "Social networking is to social, what reality television is to reality." I don't know if I'm up to the task, but I want to quibble with Sorkin. Don't get me wrong, social networking is a strange phenomenon and reality television is totally decadent. But what I think Sorkin was essentially saying is that we like to control our own reality. Facebook, he thinks, is just an edited version of social interaction and so it's not truly social, just like reality television is just an edited version of reality so it's not reality. When we shape reality, then it ceases to be reality and becomes an edited version of it—that's his take.

I disagree. Humans were created to be shapers of life. Human vocation is rooted in our co-creative potential. We were made to be fruitful and multiply, fill the earth, subdue it, have dominion over it, till it, and keep it. Humans were created to be co-creators with God. We are not victims of reality. We are free to help shape and create that reality in the way that we live our lives. We are not free to create any reality we want. My youngest son once swiped one of his older brother's Oreo cookies. When I quizzed him about whether or not this is true, he said no and wryly smiled, revealing a mouth full of nasty black Oreo-tainted teeth. We cannot create any reality we want. The key is to participate in ultimate reality, which we believe has come to us in the person of Jesus Christ.

There is a future God has destined for us to be a part of creating. We are not passively engaged in tomorrow, we are actively engaged in the creation of tomorrow. That is the human vocation envisioned by God. In our Scriptures, God reiterated it both before and after the fall of humankind. We are all born with the potential to participate in what God is doing in the world, to accomplish something bigger than ourselves.

Yet God does not force this life upon us. We have to choose it. Some things God *must* do for us. For instance, salvation is God's deal. God accomplishes this in and for us. God does this for us because we cannot do it for ourselves. But there are some things God will not do for us. He will not do them for us because *he created us to do them for ourselves*. When I was teaching my oldest son how to tie his shoes, there were often times when we were leaving the house in a hurry and I could've tied them for him and saved us the five minutes and the drama. However, tying his own shoes is something he is meant to do for the rest of his life. So we take the extra time so he can participate in something that is important for him to do. The kingdom of God is sort of like that. Our life is meant to be lived as a creative act of worship before God. It is our performance for him. We are actively engaged in the creation of God's future, it is part of what it means to be human. God empowers it, but we have to respond—God will not live our lives for us.

THE GOSPEL OF THE KINGDOM OF GOD

What I'm describing is called the gospel of the Kingdom of God. It was Jesus Christ's central message. When we tell the story of God, we must talk about cosmic redemption and the renewal of all things. We anticipate the day when God will reign and rule on earth just as God reigns and rules in heaven. This is the gospel of the Kingdom of God.

Consider Mark 1:14. Here we are told that the good news is that the Kingdom of God has come near. As Jesus began his ministry in this passage, he is very clear about what he believes the good news is. It is not getting into heaven when you die. It is the coming of the Kingdom of God. The kingdom was never very far from the lips of Jesus.

Consider Luke 8:1. When Jesus began to travel around and preach in the villages and towns, he spoke of the good news of the Kingdom of God.

Consider Luke 9:1-12. When Jesus sent out his followers he told them to proclaim the good news of the coming of the Kingdom of God.

After the resurrection Jesus appeared for forty days and had one message, the coming of the Kingdom of God. In Acts, the very last record of the Apostle Paul's life is that he welcomed all who came to him and proclaimed to them the coming of the Kingdom of God through Christ. The gospel Jesus came to enact and proclaim was that the Kingdom of God—life under the reign and rule of God—is now possible for anyone who desires it.

Kingdom is an easy concept. A kingdom is where the will of the king is done. A kingdom is where whatever the king declares is going to happen, happens. The Kingdom of God is the range in which God's will is sovereign. His kingdom has come both to the hearts of human persons and to the created order through Jesus Christ who taught us to pray: *Thy kingdom come, thy will be done on earth as it is in heaven.*

The gospel we often hear among evangelicals is sadly individualistic and fatalistic. It is individualistic because it is only about you and God, and how your sins will be atoned. It is fatalistic because it does not come to fruition until you die. The typical evangelical gospel is a gospel built for death. The gospel Jesus preached was a gospel built for life. It is not individualistic because it lives at the nexus of the person and the community. It is not fatalistic because it is not merely about what happens when you die, but about what happens now.

THE SAVING ACTIVITY OF GOD
AND THE SCOPE OF SALVATION

Rauschenbusch mused about this concept in his chapter on eschatology in *A Theology for the Social Gospel*. He was very concerned with the ways in which the future of the people of God and the *telos* of redemption were distorted in the theology of his day. He was adept at pointing out the fatalism of evangelical theology. He noted with dissatisfaction that evangelicals seem "best pleased when they see humanity defeated and collapsing, for then salvation is nigh."[1] If the plan of salvation, as many suppose, is to let the world burn while the chosen few—and I mean very few—survive, then what is the point of any kind of social action? This fatalistic view that the earth is doomed as are most of the people who have ever lived

1. Rauschenbusch, *Social Gospel*, 211.

on it has many problem, not the least of which is that it fails to recognize Jesus's chief aim was the renewal of all things and the accomplishment of God's will on earth as in heaven. Thus all who suffer from the impact of corporate sin are left with no hope.

Rauschenbusch could not stomach this approach because it did not fit with the character of God and the way God has been revealed through the Scriptures, specifically through the Old Testament prophets. The prophetic threat of judgment was always meant to act as a corrective measure. Judgment is meant to be redemptive. The prophets, Rauschenbusch believed, were shot through with the assumption that "God is in history . . . working toward redemption."[2] He firmly believed God is tirelessly, actively, whole-heartedly pursuing the redemption of all creation.

Yet, most evangelicals subscribe to a kind of "left behind" Christianity that is actually not very well backed by Scripture. Salvation is not a condemnation of the physical world and the narrow escape of our souls via the "rapture" of the church; This notion is actually very foreign to the Bible, yet it captivates the imagination of most evangelical Christians. God's saving action is always redemptive and restorative, and its scope is always the entire created order. The Scriptures teach us that creation will not be destroyed in the end. It will be redeemed and renewed, just as Christ's body was redeemed and renewed in his resurrection.

Consider Acts 3:19-21. This passage tells us that God's redemptive project is to "restore everything, as he promised long ago through his holy prophets." In his article "A New Heaven and a New Earth,"[3] Richard Middleton points out that the key to interpreting this and passages like it in the New Testament is to consider two questions: What is the saving activity of God? And what is its scope? In this verse, the saving activity is not destruction but restoration, and it is applied to everything. The scope of God's saving action is cosmic.

Consider Ephesians 1:9–10, where we are told that God has planned "to bring all things in heaven and on earth together under one head, even Christ." Here the saving action is unification under Christ, and the scope of this unification is all things in heaven and on earth.

Consider Colossians 1:19–20. Here we are told God has chosen to use Christ to "reconcile to himself all things, whether things on earth or

2. Ibid., 223.
3. Middleton, "A New Heaven," 73–97.

thing in heaven." Here the saving action is reconciliation, and the scope is again all things both on earth and in heaven.

Consider 2 Peter 3:10–13. Here the day of the Lord comes like a thief and all of creation is passed through God's cosmic smelter, to purify it and it will be laid bare. Here the saving activity of God is renewal and the scope is both heaven and earth.

Consider Romans 8:19–23, where Paul draws on the imagery of childbirth. The creation will be "liberated from its bondage to decay and brought into the glorious freedom of the children of God." All of creation groans for redemption, including all human beings who await "the redemption of our bodies." Here the saving action of God is liberation, and the scope is creation itself and all of humanity—even our bodies.

When we view all of these various texts together, we begin to see a pattern emerge. God's saving action is not the destruction of the created order, but the renewal of it. God is not doing something totally new. God is re-doing something that has gone awry. The scope of this redemptive work is described "as holistically and comprehensively as possible."[4] God's saving action is restoration, unification, reconciliation, renewal, liberation. The scope of this action is cosmic, all things in heaven and on earth, creation itself, and humanity.

Is this the gospel we hold to? Is this the story we tell with the way that we live our lives? It does not seem to be widely held or preached among evangelical Christians, and this is a huge problem. As Christians, we should be taught to believe our hope is not to win heaven and immortality; our hope is the resurrection and redemptive recreation of all things on heaven and earth through Jesus Christ. We have been invited to participate in God's redemptive mission, and we have been equipped for the task by Christ who sent the Holy Spirit to enliven and empower the church. The good news is not that the evildoers will get smashed in the end, lest we forget that we are all evildoers. The good news is that the future of God has coming rushing into the present through Jesus Christ. Heaven has invaded earth in the person of Jesus Christ, who prayed, "Thy kingdom come, Thy will be done on earth as it is in heaven."

4. Ibid., 91.

WHAT HAVE WE BEEN MISSING?

The gospel of the Kingdom of God has been lost among evangelical Christians, to our great detriment. Perhaps Rauschenbusch's greatest achievement was that he became a prophet for the rediscovery of the doctrine of the Kingdom of God. Rauschenbusch believed the church had forgotten the true nature of the Kingdom of God as the central aim of God's redemptive project. "When the doctrine of the Kingdom of God shriveled to an undeveloped and pathetic remnant in Christian thought," he wrote, "this loss was bound to have far-reaching consequences . . . the atrophy of that idea which had occupied the chief place in the mind of Jesus, necessarily affected the conception of Christianity, the life of the Church, the progress of humanity, and the structure of theology."[5]

One of the keys to his entire theological project was his explanation of the major consequences of that loss.[6] He believed when the church lost the theology of the Kingdom of God it essentially bartered away its birthright for a bowl of beans. He knew this mistake would have serious consequences in the life of the church. Rauschenbusch covered ten of those consequences in detail. He believed when the church lost the theology of the Kingdom of God many things happened:

1. Theology lost the ability to think like Jesus thought, especially regarding the Kingdom of God. The Kingdom of God was Jesus's central preoccupation. When it was lost, the church became incapable of truly understanding his life and message.

2. Jesus's ethical principles were the result of his view of the Kingdom of God. When the Kingdom of God was lost, so were the ethics of Jesus.

3. The church became a fellowship for worship instead of a fellowship of righteousness. In other words, it became about belief and not about being.

4. When Kingdom of God ceased to "be the dominating religious reality,"[7] the church took its place and claimed supremacy. The result was that the church became enticed and corrupted by its own power, and ultimately it began to participate, and in some

---

5. Rauschenbusch, *Social Gospel*, 133.

6. These are condensed from the larger section in which Rauschenbusch goes into much more detail (ibid., 133–38).

7. Ibid., 134.

cases to serve, the Kingdom of Evil. Rauschenbusch cited as proof the reality that the Kingdom of God cannot be promoted "by lies, craft, crime or war," while the "wealth and power of the Church have often been promoted by these means."[8]

5. The Kingdom of God is the test and corrective ideal of the church. Without it the church hasn't a proper conscience. Therefore the church became a partner in unjust social conditions without the slightest conviction of her corporate sins and her duty to oppose them.

6. The Kingdom of God is the revolutionary force of the church. Without this revolutionary force, the church supported whatever power structures were already in place in a given culture and thus, the church became unable to critique injustice to any effective measure.

7. Movements for mercy and social justice were left without adequate spiritual backing from the church. They became something ancillary, added on like a program, instead of something central to the church's very existence.

8. Civic service and secular life were then belittled compared with service to the church, as the religious character of common everyday life ceased its prophetic role to society. The concept of the church as a missional entity died out and mission became a sub-program within the larger church.

9. Relationship between the salvation of the individual and the redemption of the social order was fractured as the whole affair gave way to individualism. The corporate nature of the Christian faith became completely incoherent and eventually lost altogether.

10. Theology was deprived of the inspiration of great ideas contained in the Kingdom of God ideal. "The Kingdom of God breeds prophets; the church breeds priests and theologians,"[9] who run to traditionalism and dogma. Christianity became about conforming to cultural norms that were simply baptized with religious language. Thus the church lost its ability to renew culture—to

8. Ibid., 135.
9. Ibid., 137.

participate in the renewal, restoration, and reconciliation of all creation, and instead condemned creation to death.

The doctrine of the Kingdom of God Rauschenbusch puts forward is meant to be the teleology of the entire faith because that is what Jesus himself taught! The Kingdom is both present and future, "always coming, always pressing in on the present, always big with possibility, and always inviting immediate action."[10] It is a vision of "humanity organized according to the will of God."[11]

Thus it demands something of all of us. It demands that we press for a just social order. It demands that there be progress in the love of God and neighbor, not just with individual persons, but in the way we organize our common life together. This love finds its highest expression when its members begin to hold in common those things the super-personal forces of evil urge us to grasp and hoard, i.e., money, property, capital, personal rights, affluence, power, and control. This progressive reign of love should move each person toward the "other" in ever increasing unity.

This, of course, is the vision of Jesus when he proclaims the year of the Lord's favor in Luke 4. Jesus's vision of the Kingdom of God was Jubilee, which required Israel to compel its citizens to hold the land in common once again. This served as a social correction to any who might have spent the previous forty-nine years grasping for money, property, capital, etc. What Jesus describes in Luke 4 is what Rauschenbusch was calling for—humanity to organize its common life together according to the will of God, so that they can image God to all creation. Luke 4, therefore, becomes a crucial text for this view of social redemption. For it is not the church, the people of Israel, or any of us who will bring about this radical new situation Jesus describes. *Jesus himself* is bringing this to pass.

Rauschenbusch has too often been critiqued for having far too much confidence in the human ability to realize the kingdom of God, which is often called the myth of progress. Although this accusation has some merit, it is not the case in his doctrine of the Kingdom of God. Rauschenbusch characteristically began his explanation of the doctrine of the Kingdom of God by affirming its divine origin. He saw it as initiated

10. Ibid., 141.

11. Ibid., 142.

by Christ in Luke 4, won in his faithful life, death, and resurrection, sustained by the power of the Holy Spirit, and advanced solely by the power of God as God works through the lives of human beings. He understood that the Kingdom of Evil was so powerful in this world that it had captivated the imagination of most people. This captivation was so powerful it blinded most people to the transcendent nature of the Kingdom of God. He believed only the active influx of energy and purpose from above, not human effort, could advance the kingdom. He wrote, "The Kingdom of God, therefore, is miraculous all the way, and is the continuous revelation of the power, the righteousness, and the love of God. The establishment of a community of righteousness in mankind is just as much a saving act of God as the salvation of an individual from his natural selfishness and moral inability. The Kingdom of God, therefore, is not merely ethical, but has a rightful place in theology."[12]

Typical treatments of Rauschenbusch seldom resist the tendency to caricature his position then dismiss it as failed nineteenth century liberalism. But, *perhaps the problem is not that Rauschenbusch valued human effort too much, but his critics value the ability of the human person to participate in the transcendent and miraculous nature of the Kingdom of God too little*. A fuller understanding of his doctrine of the Kingdom will reveal his confidence was not in human effort but in the transcendent and miraculous nature of the Kingdom of God. He spurned the notion that the Kingdom of God should be equated with the church. God is free to work with any super-personal force God chooses. *The Kingdom does not come by human effort but will not come without it*. From start to finish, the Kingdom comes through Jesus Christ.

12. Ibid., 139–40.

10 Finding Faith

"It is by grace we are saved through faith"[1] could be the most used and abused text from the Bible. Paul was saying something incredibly important, but we often make Paul say things he did not mean. The conviction that we are saved by grace through faith is a major tenet of Protestant Christianity. Salvation is meritless; it is sheer gratuity; it is a gift we can only gratefully receive. We do no generate it, earn it, or acquire it in any way. Salvation happens by the grace of God, this is a pillar of what it means to be an evangelical. It comes through faith—and this is where the problem lies.

FAITH IS A BIG WORD

Faith is a big word for the Christian. We are saved through faith.[2] We walk by faith not by sight.[3] We have one Lord, one faith, and one baptism.[4] Faith set us free from the custody of the law.[5] We are justified by faith.[6] The Greek word Paul uses in each of these cases is *pistis*, which we translate as faith. The word faith, especially in evangelicalism, is generally understood as trust or belief. However, trust or belief does not come anywhere close to exhausting the meaning of the word *pistis* as it was used by the apostle Paul.

The word *pistis* carries with it a whole complex of meanings: trust, belief, faith, faithfulness, love, fidelity, devotion, total commitment, or what N.T. Wright calls "believing allegiance."[7] Wright's new wording is

1. Ephesians 2:8, (NIV).
2. Ephesians 2:8.
3. 2 Corinthians 5:7.
4. Ephesians 4:5.
5. Galatians 3:23.
6. Romans 3:30.
7. Wright, "New Perspectives on Paul," 256.

helpful because the modern English word "faith" simply does not get the job done. Faith certainly implies trust, but it is an active trust which is much closer to the meaning of the word fidelity.

Belief is a slippery concept. Just imagine you are pulled over by a police officer for driving seventy-five where the limit is fifty-five miles per hour. He asks you why you were driving so fast. Would you say, "I know the speed limit is only fifty-five, I believe that in my heart. In fact, I was going fifty-five in my heart; it's just that I was in a hurry on the outside!" Once the officer stops laughing, you're going to get a ticket. Faith is like that. It's not simply an inner phenomenon. Faith must be active or else it is not faith.

Fidelity in marriage is a trust and commitment lives in the heart of each person. But fidelity of the heart is useless if the spouse has an affair. If you say to your husband, "I love you with all of my heart," when he has just found you in bed with another man, your profession of single-minded love—or fidelity—would be a lie. Fidelity has to work itself out in real life. Faith is like that. The concepts of fidelity and believing allegiance are both typically involved when Paul speaks of the faith of the believer. They must be held alongside the standard definition of faith as trust or belief in order to approach the field of meaning upon which Paul drew.

We already acknowledge the definition of faith as "believing allegiance" in many ways within our typical churches. In fact we acknowledge it much more in our practice than in our theology. People typically can't be deacons or elders if they have a pattern of divorcing their wives or husbands when things get rough. It's understood that faith in Christ involves the ability to live with loyalty and fidelity in every area of life. Pastors who gossip or live with continual habits of selfishness lose the respect of the congregation and become ineffective because their professions of faith do not bear out in their lives.

One cannot profess to have faith in Christ and continually break faith with Christ. In our theology, evangelicals have long considered faith to be equated with belief or trust, but in reality we already acknowledge a much broader meaning. The concept of faith must never come to mean less than belief that Jesus is the Messiah and the Son of God who paid the price for our sins and purchased our pardon through his blood. But it must come to mean more than that. We must not ignore the element of belief and trust involved in faith, but we must begin to acknowledge the element of faithfulness, fidelity, loyalty, and believing allegiance involved when Paul uses the word *pistis*.

It has been my assertion all along here that individualized theology is problematic at nearly every turn. Nowhere is this more important than in our discussion of faith. Personal faith is extremely important. People must trust Christ in the deepest recesses of their hearts and experience the personal renewal that comes from faith. Yet the faith of the Christian does not happen in a vacuum. It has a corporate element as well. Rauschenbusch wrote, "Faith is an energetic act of the will, affirming our fellowship with God and man, declaring our solidarity with the Kingdom of God, and repudiating selfish isolation."[8] Faith is actually part of what binds our hearts together as a church. Faith not only reaches up, but reaches out; otherwise it is not a robust faith, but a sterile belief system that may or may not bear fruit for the kingdom.

Not only is there a corporate element to faith, but it is corporately mediated at every turn. Faith is a gift that comes to us from the community of the faithful. Where did you learn about Jesus? Who told you about his love? Who invited you to follow him? Who taught you what that meant? Who modeled faith to you and helped you to take your first steps toward it? None of these things happen in a vacuum. The community of faith came and found you. They made the body of Christ present to you. You received your faith from a church because churches have a living and active faith. Faith defines them and they are sustained by it. They are saved and are being saved by faith that is corporate as well as personal. Personal faith must be nurtured by a community of faith for it to survive. Personal faith will not live long without connection to a corporate community of faith. If your faith has been passed on to another—your friends, your family, or your children—then you have experienced the corporate nature of faith firsthand. Faith must be corporate and active for personal faith to pass from one generation to another.

There is a corporate faith that keeps personal faith from running headlong into ill advised actions or doctrinal peril. Corporate faith and personal faith need one another. The healthiest place to be, in terms of faith, is the nexus of the corporate and the personal. I see this play itself out most often in decisions that are termed personal, yet have tremendous impact on the body of Christ. As a pastor, nothing is more painful

8. Rauschenbusch, *Social Gospel*, 102.

than watching families break fellowship with our congregation. When people leave, scars are left behind because they are breaking faith. They are violating the corporate nature of faith. I often tell our congregation that faithful participation in the mission of God is not dependent upon our ability to have the right answers to the right question, nor is it dependent upon our ability to have our doctrines all perfectly in place. Our faithful participation in the mission of God is dependent upon our ability to keep faith with one another and with God; to stick together and not leave each other, come what may. Faith in Christ is loyalty, faithfulness, fidelity, trust, believing allegiance *both to God and the part of the body of Christ to which we belong.*

I've noticed a pattern within this phenomenon. People who tell me they are leaving our church always begin the decision with the same three words: "We have decided." By the time those words are uttered, faith has already been broken. These are some of the most painful words I ever have to hear. "We have decided to leave for this or that reason." The reasons they give vary and they usually have at least some merit. Yet they pale in comparison to the egregious sin of breaking fellowship—read faith, fidelity, faithfulness, allegiance, *pistis*—with that part of the body of Christ to which they have been given. This is one of the most insidious forms of individualism. Why do people feel as though they can make the decision to leave their community of faith in private, without ever submitting this decision to the rest of the body? In truth this action violates the unity of the body. It runs counter to the notion that our worship runs much deeper than simply where we go to church on Sunday. Rather worship involves the whole of our lives. To "decide" privately to leave a church means we sever deep bonds of friendship and community that are meant to be reciprocal relationships. The phrase, "We have decided," is a sign that individualism has so pervaded our lives and our Christian faith that we think we are fully justified in making decisions on behalf of everyone in our community without consulting them. This, I believe, is one of the most damaging effects of individualism on the church.

What is most tragic to know as a pastor is this: if a family or person will bring the decision to the body, the body will generally heal whatever the hurt is that has them considering leaving. And if the hurt cannot be healed, or if another kind of decision is in play—such as moving to a different town for work or finding a church with a different focus—then typically the body affirms the decision to leave as a calling from God.

When this happens there is no scar after the people have left. The community can affirm that God has called them to a different place, lay hands on them, affirm their decision, and send them out even if they are sending them out to a church right across the street. If faith is merely a personal thing, then one can say "we have decided" anytime they wish. If faith is corporate as well, then to say "we have decided" does violence to the unity of the body and to the corporate faith.

MISSIONAL GOD, MISSIONAL COMMUNITY

We are saved by grace through faith, which is to be understood as faithfulness, fidelity, trust, and believing allegiance. When we are saved by grace through faith it is for a specific purpose. This purpose actually begins to define us as persons and as the people of God. The purpose becomes both what we are and what we are to do. This purpose is called the *missio dei*, or the mission of God.

God is a missional God. What this actually means can be a bit complicated, and it is not widely understood among evangelicals. Most of us have been nurtured to believe as Zizioulas says, "first you are, and then you relate."[9] First we exist, then we find something to do with our lives. We get this belief about ourselves because we have believed it to be the way God is as well. As a result there exists a bifurcation between our "being" and our "mission," and this is problematic. In laypersons terms, this is how it works. God exists as Trinity—a community of ecstatic love. God's very being is love. This is why the Scripture says God is love. The Scripture does not say God is, therefore, God loves; it says God—at the heart of it all—is love. God's mission is love and God's being is love, therefore *God's being is God's mission*. Mission isn't something *derived* from God's character, mission *is* God's character. Mission is not derived at all. Mission is the way God exists, it is ontological. This is what it means to say God is love.

Just as we derive our personal being from God, we derive our corporate being from God as well. The church does not, strictly speaking, have its own mission. God has a cosmic mission of love and redemption. It is this mission that calls the church into being. Our being is God's mission of redemption to which we have been called. The church derives its identity, true purpose, and meaning from the very nature of its missional

---

9. Zizioulas, *Being as Communion*, 103.

God. As such, the church is a contingent entity, completely reliant upon God's grace and energy. Thus, the church's nature follows after the nature of God. Just as God is a missional God, the church is missional as well.

What is a missional church? The church is supposed to be unlike anything else on earth—it's not a club, it's not a school, it's not a team, it's not philosophy, it's really not even a religion—at least it's not *just* a religion. When Jesus went to be with God, he didn't leave behind any of those things. He left the church—a people—a *peculiar people*. They were to be a people of mission.

In church leadership circles it's sort of assumed any church, group, or team needs to have a mission. So people write mission statements, vision statements, or purpose statements. I actually have no clue what the differences between those things are. I have friends with MBAs who try to tell me the difference and either I'm too dumb to get the difference or they are too sly to admit there really is no difference. My question is simply, "What's the main thing? What are you really about?" And it's hardly ever what is written on the wall or the website; it's not what's on the banners or the stationary. The main thing is what you really do—not just what you talk about doing, but what you actually really do. That's what your mission, vision, or purpose really is.

For the church it's really not that hard. We don't really have a mission. God has a mission and God's mission calls the church into existence. What we are supposed to do is to pour ourselves out *for the life of the world*. We're supposed to humble ourselves and empty ourselves for others. Now, something like that doesn't just happen. That's just not how things work in our culture. The world we live in is all about being upwardly mobile. More is better, enough is never enough, and whatever you've got, you should enjoy it and hold on to it. But the church is supposed to be different. This is what Jesus meant when he said, "If you try to find your life, you will lose it; but if you lose your life for my sake, you will find it." How does that happen?

The best metaphor I know of for how this works itself out practically is the concept of breathing. Every week God breathes his church into his lungs. It's a cosmic inhalation that draws the church together every seven days. What happens when the church gathers is of great importance. We gather together around the word and the table to be shaped by God who holds us in his lungs and empowers the entire thing himself. The people of God gather, first and foremost, around the story of God—the

Scriptures—and they tell and retell the story in the most creative and imaginative ways possible. Over time they begin to see themselves as living in that story—not the story of our culture, but the story of God—it comes to define them as a people more than any other rival story. We say that the rival stories—individualism, consumerism, nationalism, and stuff like that—those stories can't tell us who we really are. Those stories can't really help us make sense of what we have been created to be, why we are here, and where we are going. The only story that makes sense of it all is God's story. And so we give ourselves over to the story of God and begin to organize our common life together in such a way that we can be faithful to that story. In my community we call it transformation. Whatever you want to call it, it is the process through which God draws the church into God's lungs and shapes us and forms us, enriches us and prunes us. This process is thoroughly corporate and yet always very personal.

Then God exhales. He blows us out of his lungs and into the world. As little transformed agents of redemption we are sent out into the places we always go—our home, our schools, our workplaces, our neighborhoods, our families, etc. We go there as salt and light. We go there as people who do not walk by sight but by faith—*pistis*—believing allegiance. We are transformed vessels of God's redemption sent to season all of creation. We image God. So, when people look at us they actually see past us, and get a good look at God. We become caught up in the love of God and become transformed into the kind of people who go out into the world as salt and light and actually image God to all creation because we're image-bearing people.

And if we participate in this breathing, an amazing thing happens in a church like that. The Bible calls it redemption. When redemption happens, each person begins to relate to God's creation the way God planned it from the beginning. Redemption happens in the way we relate to God, the self, other people, and to all creation. Little by little as we are being transformed—i.e., switching narratives from the narratives of individualism, nationalism, and consumerism to the narrative of the Story of God—redemption advances upon creation. And the Scriptures promise us that as the just begin to live by faith, the gates of hell cannot stand against the coming Kingdom of God. In other words, in the end, love wins because God is love.

A lot of people think the pastor's job is to make a church survive, or thrive, or get bigger, or be better, but that's not a pastor's job. Those sorts of things are best left up to God. In fact, I'd be a little wary of any pastor who thought they could deliver on those promises. Because that's not the church's job—the church isn't supposed to *survive*—the church is supposed to be *faithful*. And faithfulness takes on many forms, but most of the time it sort of looks like dying: dying to ourselves, dying to each other, dying a little bit every day for our family, friends, neighbors, co-workers, and all of humanity. But we know with death comes a resurrection. And resurrection is the great hope of our faith. I think that's how the church works.

RIVAL GODS

This way of being the church is not without opposition. There is a whole complex of rival gods at work in Western culture. They attempt to tell us who we are and what our mission is, but they are ultimately doomed to failure. The most prominent rival gods in American culture are the gods of individualism, nationalism, and consumerism. These gods exercise sovereignty over the lives of most people. Much of the evangelical faith has become a form of some combination of individualism, nationalism, and consumerism baptized with religious (Christian) language. We worship these rival gods with our tithes and offerings. They exercise sovereignty over us. They lead and guide our decisions and define us as persons and as a society. Yet they are false gods. They cannot tell us who we are and why we are here. They can only confuse and deceive us and how we understand ourselves.

These gods are reinforced by the liturgy of our culture. The liturgy of culture is enacted, for the most part, via television and internet media marketing. Marketing is built on a two-step process. First, marketers make you feel like what you have is not good enough. Second, they tell you why purchasing their product will be better than what you have. What is never said is the reality that undergirds the situation: stuff makes a lousy god. Stuff has no power to help us with our lives. Stuff can only distract us from who we really are. Consumerism is a lousy god. The same goes for nationalism and individualism. Individuals make lousy gods and so do nations. We are told we are a people of rights and freedoms, and that our individualism is sovereign. We are told that America is the great shining city on a hill, God's chosen nation. It's simply a false narrative, but a narrative pushed on us at every turn by a culture that has learned how to profit from it. In the end it is a failed story—a bad narrative. It cannot help us to live in peace.

There is only one way to counteract the rival gods of the culture. We must name them as idols and renounce them to be sure, but that will not break their backs. In order to de-throne the rival gods of our culture we must patiently, persistently articulate an alternative narrative over years and years. We must give ourselves over to an alternative narrative—the story of God. This happens only in community. It happens as the people of God enact counter-liturgies to those of the culture. When we give ourselves to a community that has a different mode of being than the rest of the world, we can be shaped and formed by the story of God. The story of God stands diametrically opposed to the gods of individualism, consumerism, and nationalism; it is fully committed to the Kingdom of God. This is why the definition of faith as believing allegiance is so important. This is why it is so important to understand the metaphor of the church as being breathed in by God each week—transformed and shaped—then breathed out into the world as salt and light. This is why faith cannot be simply a belief system. It has to be experienced as a way of being that images God and draws us into God's mission. Tragically, most people are enslaved to a rival story that tells them powerful lies about who they really are.

I think we are very confused about what it means to be human. In particular, we are confused about the nature of personhood. Not only have we given ourselves to the false god of individualism, but we have forgotten why we were created in the first place. We were created to worship God with the way we live our lives—personally and corporately—and in so doing, we image God to all creation. Our lives are meant to be an act of creative worship wherein we pour ourselves out for the life of the world.

CONTAINER V. FUNNEL

This complex of rival gods—the unholy trinity—has convinced many evangelicals that what we essentially are is a container. God pours out his blessings upon us and our job is to soak them up. From the day we are born God pours resources into our lives. At first they are simple: a womb, nourishment from a mother, and basic safety. Most of us received incredible gifts from God when we were young: a family, food, shelter, clothing, love, support, and nurture. Most of us received an education, and the example of role models. We were the beneficiaries of countless modes of support, opportunity, and resources. The Christian story tells us that these are all gifts from God. Even simple things like health, friendships, and physical vitality are to be received as a gift. We also receive material resources, talents, and abilities. These are all gifts. Out of those gifts we can work to create things like careers, incomes, retirement accounts, and savings accounts. We can buy houses and cars, cell phones and game systems. We can have children and families. Whether we realize it or not, God is at the center of all of this as its source. Yet, even if we agree that all of life is to be received as a gift, most American Christians are extremely confused as to what sort of vessel these blessings have been poured into. We mistakenly view ourselves as a container.

Most of us think we are a container, as though God pours these resources into us and our job is to protect them at all costs. The container is a lousy metaphor for the person.[10] It is about keeping God's blessings to ourselves. It is about survival. When God pours his blessing into a container, and the container is plopped down in a world that is about a mile wide and an inch deep, the container does nothing. It just keeps everything inside and has no impact on the culture at large. The container-person is useless to the Kingdom of God.

Humans are not containers, we are funnels. Everything that comes into our lives is meant to flow out the other side. God pours his resources into our lives not so we can contain them, but so we can steward them into the rest of the world. You plop a funnel down into a world that is a mile wide and an inch deep, and as God pours resources through them and into the rest of the world, you've got yourself a kingdom building machine. This is how the kingdom comes. We are not containers, we are funnels. God is the source of all of life, our gifts, talents, resources, income, abilities, passions, etc. Our job is not to leverage those to keep our container full. Our job is to let them flow freely through our lives into the lives of others, believing that the source will never dry up.

This is not only who we are in this life, but this is who we will always be, even in the life to come. We will live on into eternity as funnels of the very life-giving presence of God. On the other side of this life, we will see

---

10. When we are called earthen vessels or jars of clay (2 Cor. 4:7), this is meant to convey the temporary nature of our bodies, not that we are in some sense a container. It just means mortal bodies that are passing or being used up, which supports what I'm saying here. The light on the lamp-stand also fits with the funnel analogy. Here we are to be burned up completely so that the world can come to see the light.

the source face to face. As God continues to pour life and light into our lives we will allow it to flow through us and into all of creation, and this will go on forever and forever. But on this side, we cannot see the source. That is why we need faith. That is also why we need each other. I need other people to remind me that God is the source of all of life and that the source will never run dry. The funnel is missional, the container is not.

Ultimately, the goal of life is to die empty, having exhausted ourselves for the life of the world. This is how the kingdom comes. This is the way of Jesus. The unbelievable blessing of living this way of life is that God's blessings never run dry.

Individualism tells you that you deserve to have what you want. Consumerism tells you that you can buy it at the corner mall. Nationalism says when you buy it, you should by American. None of those things come anywhere close to the abundant life God offers. Only the way of self-emptying is the way of Jesus. Only the way of self-emptying can help us to live lives which are truly satisfying and peaceful. The reason is that this is how God has made creation to be. When we partake in this way of life, we participate with how God has made creation to be at its very core.

The church is not a container either. The church is a funnel. Our job as the church of Christ is not to survive. Our job is to empty ourselves on behalf of the world. Our job is to die empty, just like Jesus did.

11 What Kind of Story Are You In?

In the movie *Stranger Than Fiction*, Will Ferrell plays a character named Harold Crick, who wakes up one day to the voice of a narrator in his head. This narrator is telling a story in which Harold is the main character. Everything the narrator says is going to happen really happens to Harold, so you can imagine his alarm when the narrator predicts his impending demise. Stunned and desperate, Harold eventually seeks out a literature professor (played by Dustin Hoffman), for advice as to how he should deal with this particular malady. Hoffman tells his new friend that there are only two kinds of stories, a comedy or a tragedy. In a comedy the hero gets the girl, in a tragedy, the hero dies. What Harold Crick must do is find out what kind of story he is in. I think this is one of the most confusing things for Christians to wrap their minds around. The story of God is not bound by these kinds of rules. Our story is not simply a comedy or a tragedy. It is both. In fact, the story of Jesus teaches us that the hero, metaphorically speaking, "gets the girl" only by dying (which is sort of how it happens for Harold Crick as well).

What kind of story do you think you are living in? Because of the life, death, and resurrection of Jesus, we know what kind of story we are living in. Yet, the ways in which most of us talk about the story of God and attempt to live it out in our daily lives are very confused. We don't know what kind of story we are living in. So we uncritically accept the story we are fed by the culture through its weak and distorted folk theology. In the end, the only effective disciples will be those who have received a vision of the kingdom of God and leveraged all of their life and resources to surrender themselves to its realization by grace through faith. And this is not a way to prosperity and riches, it is a way to peace—and it only comes through the cruciform life (the life which actually takes on the shape of the cross). The good news has come to us and is still coming to us through Jesus, and it is having a profound impact upon the world. The Kingdom of God comes in power every time some little community of faith figures out what kind of story they are living in. Once they do, and once they allow Jesus's vision of the Kingdom of God to define them over and against all of the rival stories thrust upon them by the culture, they become a part of God's salvation. When this happens, look out. Transformation is not far behind.

THE IMPACT OF MISSIONAL COMMUNITY

I have a friend named Bob. Bob is a homeless man who has been an alcoholic for about a decade. He lives in a tent back in the woods under a bridge in town. Bob had a hard life and experienced a lot of pain growing up. As an adult, he was in the armed forces and fought in Somalia. He saw some terrible things happen to his friends. As a result of these traumatic experiences Bob has post-traumatic stress disorder. His way of coping has been to drink himself into a coma pretty much every day for a decade. He lost his job and his family. He wound up living under a bridge, drinking away every penny he had.

Bob is my friend because two members of my church, Jim and Jennifer, started going to feed him and a bunch of other homeless people twice a week. They work with an organization in Kansas City called Uplift. Uplift takes food and provisions to the hard-core homeless. These are the people who cannot come into the shelters because they are typically still using some sort of substance and living in a self-destructive pattern. They cannot come to ministries and shelters because they are too addicted and destructive. They couldn't come to church, so my friends took the church to them in the form of hot food and clothing. That is missional behavior.

Over several years of involvement, Jim and Jennifer came to be friends with Bob. They prayed with him when he needed prayer and they talked with him about God and why they were feeding him each week. After awhile, Bob began asking them if they could bring him to church. So, they started doing so. Pretty soon there were a couple others asking as well, so they brought them, too. Each week Jim or Jennifer, or someone else from our church will drive downtown—a 30 minute drive each way—and pick up Bob and a few of his friends and bring them to a place called Redemption. Here they are welcomed as Christ and invited to participate in the body of Christ.

One day Bob stopped drinking. He just stopped. Nobody talked to him about it, nobody asked him to. He just did it cold turkey. When we asked him why, he told us about a time in our church service just a few weeks earlier when Jim had shared about dealing with his own past addictions. Jim simply witnessed to the redemptive power of Jesus, his pursuit of the Kingdom of God, and how it he had experienced healing in his own life. It was this healing that prompted him to serve the homeless in the first place. As I write this, Bob has been sober for four months. I don't know if he'll remain like this, or if he'll ever make it off the streets, but I know that Bob is experiencing redemption today. He is being drawn up into the mission of God, and he makes our church a holy place every time he walks through the doors.

This is how mission works. Bob is being healed because the church was breathed out by God and went to find Bob. Then Bob was breathed back into God's lungs with us and is being healed not by the words we say, but by the presence of God in his church. Bob receives the body and blood of Jesus each and every week and it is healing him from the inside out. Our church is no great shakes. We are not that innovative and we are small. Nobody will sponsor leadership events to try and see how we are doing things in order to copy us. But we are participating in God's redemption. We are fighting back the darkness because of the way we organize our common life together. Each week God breathes us into his lungs and shapes and forms us. God infuses us with his presence and then sends us out in the world as salt and light. We bear witness to God's redemption all week long in our homes, neighborhoods, workplaces, and anywhere we go. Then he draws us back into his lungs the next week, and on it goes.

WHAT KIND OF STORY ARE YOU IN?

At Redemption we often say that we don't go to Redemption Church, we are Redemption Church. We take Redemption with us everywhere we go. Our mission is not to get people to come to our church; our mission is the person sitting next to us—everywhere. Our church has taken this idea seriously. We are not polished; in fact we screw something up nearly every Sunday morning. Our sound system is always having some sort of glitch. The air-conditioning is always too high or too low (or non-existent). Our musicians over-sleep and miss church. Our presentation is far from flawless. Our doctrine is not unimpeachable. Our people are ragamuffins through and through. But we have made ourselves available to God; and God is using us. We have chosen not to claim our rights as individuals, but to cling to our identity as part of the communion of saints.

You have a choice. What story do you want to live in? Do you want to live in the story of individualism? Do you want to bow to the unholy trinity of individualism, consumerism, and nationalism? Do you want to live in the story of "my information about God is better than your information about God?" Do you want to go to the church of "we are right and you are wrong," or do you want to embrace the call of Jesus who says come and die with me? Only then will you learn what it means to truly live. What kind of story do you want to live in?

Whatever you choose, the story remains the same. Your decision will determine whether you live a life in step with ultimate reality or at odds with it. Living at odds with ultimate reality is the way of death. If you choose the way of Jesus, you choose the way of life, and you are given a mission. Your mission is the person next to you, wherever you may be. Your job is to bear witness to them by being the hands and feet of Jesus. Your job is not to fight and scrap yourself to the top of the cultural heap. Your job is not to collect, hoard, accumulate, or even survive. Your job is to die empty, having given the last full measure of devotion to the lowly and forgotten people of the world. Then when you wash up on the other side, the one who made you will pick up your broken body and breathe the breath of life back into your lungs. He will renew your body and welcome you to new creation. Having died with Christ you will share in his resurrection. This is how the kingdom comes.

Bibliography

Associated Press. "Revenge of the Lug Nut." *The Seattle Times* (November 12, 2007). No pages. Online: http://seattletimes.nwsource.com/html/localnews/2004009272_web lugnut 12m.html.

Beckley, Harlan. *Passion for Justice: Retrieving the Legacies of Walter Rauschenbusch, John A. Ryan, and Reinhold Niebuhr.* Louisville: Westminster John Knox, 1992.

Berkman, John, and Cartwright, Michael, eds. *The Hauerwas Reader.* Durham, NC: Duke University Press, 2001.

Biddle, Mark. *Missing The Mark: Sin and its Consequences in Biblical Theology.* Nashville: Abingdon, 2005.

Bowman, Matthew. "Sin, Spirituality, and Primitivism: The Theologies of the American Social Gospel, 1885–1917." *Religion and American Culture* 17 (Winter 2007) 96–126.

Camp, Lee. *Mere Discipleship: Radical Christianity in a Rebellious World.* Grand Rapids: Brazos, 2003.

Cavanaugh, William T. *Torture and Eucharist.* Malden, MA: Blackwell, 1998.

Emerson, Michael O., and Smith, Christian. *Divided by Faith: Evangelical Religion and the Problem of Race in America.* New York: Oxford University Press, 2000.

Evans, Christopher H. *The Kingdom Is Always But Coming: A Life of Walter Rauschenbusch.* Waco: Baylor University Press, 2010.

Hauerwas, Stanley. *A Better Hope: Resources for a Church Confronting Capitalism, Democracy, and Postmodernity.* Grand Rapids: Brazos, 2000.

———. *Sanctify Them in the Truth: Holiness Exemplified.* Nashville: Abingdon, 1998.

———. "The Democratic Policing of Christianity." *Pro Ecclesia* 3 (Spring 1994) 215–31.

Wright, N.T. "New Perspectives on Paul." In *Justification in Perspective: Historical Developments and Contemporary Challenges,* edited by Bruce L. McCormack, 243–64. Grand Rapids: Baker Academic, 2006.

Lasch, Christopher. "Religious Contributions to Social Movement: Walter Rauschenbusch, the Social Gospel, and its Critics." *Journal of Religious Ethics* 18 (Spring 1990) 7–25.

LoBaido, Anthony C. "In search of Mary Magdalene." *WorldNetDaily.com,* February 5, 2001. Online: http://www.wnd.com/?pageId=8039.

McKnight, Scot. *A Community Called Atonement.* Nashville: Abingdon Press, 2007.

Middleton, J. Richard. "A New Heaven and a New Earth: The Case for a Holistic Reading of the Biblical Story of Redemption." *Journal for Christian Theological Research* 11 (2006) 73–97.

Minus, Paul. *Walter Rauschenbusch: American Reformer.* New York, Macmillan, 1988.

Niebuhr, Reinhold. "Walter Rauschenbusch in Historical Perspective." *Religion in Life* 27 (Autumn 1958) 52–536.

Rauschenbusch, Walter. *Christianity and the Social Crisis*. New York: Macmillan, 1907. Reprint, Louisville: Westminster John Knox, 1991.

―――. *Christianizing the Social Order*. New York: Macmillan, 1912.

―――. *A Gospel for the Social Awakening*. New York: Haddam House, 1950.

―――. *The Social Principles of Jesus*. New York: The Women's Press, 1916.

―――. *A Theology for the Social Gospel*. Louisville: John Knox, 1997.

Sharpe, Dores Robinson. *Walter Rauschenbusch*. New York: Macmillan, 1942.

Sider, Ronald. *The Scandal of the Evangelical Conscience: Why are Christians Living Just Like the Rest of the World?* Grand Rapids: Baker, 2005.

Smith, James K.A. *Introducing Radical Orthodoxy: Mapping a Post-Secular Theology*. Grand Rapids: Baker Academic, 2004.

Smucker, Dovovan E. *The Origins of Walter Rauschenbusch's Social Ethics*. Buffalo: McGill-Queen's University Press, 1994.

Warren, Rick. "Myths of the Megachurch." Speech given at the *Pew Forum's Faith Angle Conference on Religion, Politics, and Public Life*. Key West, Florida, May 2005.

Wentz, Richard. *Religion in the New World: The Shaping of Religious Traditions in the United States*. Minneapolis: Fortress, 1990.

Wiles, Maurice, and Mark Santer, eds. *Documents in Early Christian Thought*. New York: Cambridge University Press, 1975.

Willard, Dallas. *The Divine Conspiracy: Rediscovering Our Hidden Life in God*. New York: Harper Collins, 1998.

Yoder, John Howard. *The Politics of Jesus*. Grand Rapids: Eerdmans, 1994.

Zizioulas, John D. *Being as Communion*. Crestwood, NY: SVS Press, 1985.